NUREG--0917

DE82 906402

NUREG-0917

Nuclear Regulatory Commission Staff Computer Programs for Use with Meteorological Data

Manuscript Completed: June 1982
Date Published: July 1982

W. Snell

Division of Systems Integration
Office of Nuclear Reactor Regulation
U.S. Nuclear Regulatory Commission
Washington, D.C. 20555

ABSTRACT

The Nuclear Regulatory Commission (NRC) receives hour-by-hour meteorological
data on magnetic tape in a format specified in Regulatory Guide 1.70, Revision 2,
"Standard Format and Content of Safety Analysis Reports for Nuclear Power
Plants" (September 1975). The purpose of this report was to document the
computer programs that are used by the NRC meteorology staff to examine,
assess and utilize these hourly values of meteorological data. A description
of each of the programs is given along with the input requirements, discussion
of output, subroutine flow chart, a description of each subroutine, sample
output and a program listing.

TABLE OF CONTENTS

Page

1.0 Introduction 1

2.0 Background 2
     2.1 Blank Data Fields 2
     2.2 Erroneous Data 2

3.0 Program DATE (Checks for sequencial data set by date) 3
     3.1 Description of Program 3
     3.2 Input Cards 3
     3.3 Discussion of Output 3
     3.4 Implementation 3
     3.5 Subroutine Flow Chart 3
     3.6 Subroutine Descriptions 3
     3.7 Sample Output 4

4.0 Program JFREQ (Computes joint frequency distribution of wind
     speed, wind direction and atmospheric stability) 8
     4.1 Description of Program 8
     4.2 Input Cards 8
     4.3 Discussion of Output 9
     4.4 Implementation 9
     4.5 Subroutine Flow Chart 10
     4.6 Subroutine Descriptions 10
     4.7 Sample Output 12

5.0 Program MISS (Calculates missing data statistics) 24
     5.1 Description of Program 24
     5.2 Input Cards 24
     5.3 Discussion of Output 24
     5.4 Implementation 24
     5.5 Subroutine Flow Chart 24
     5.6 Subroutine Descriptions 24
     5.7 Sample Output 26

6.0 Program PRECP (Calculates precipitation statistics) 29
     6.1 Description of Program 29
     6.2 Input Cards 29
     6.3 Discussion of Output 29
     6.4 Implementation 29
     6.5 Subroutine Flow Chart 29
     6.6 Subroutine Descriptions 30
     6.7 Sample Output 31

7.0 Program PRINT (Creates listing of data) 36
     7.1 Description of Program 36
     7.2 Input Cards 36
     7.3 Discussion of Output 36
     7.4 Implementation 36
     7.5 Subroutine Flow Chart 37
     7.6 Subroutine Descriptions 37
     7.7 Sample Output 38

Table of Contents (continued)

Page

8.0   Program QA (Checks data set for invalid data values) 45
      8.1 Description of Program 45
      8.2 Input Cards 45
      8.3 Discussion of Output 46
      8.4 Implementation 46
      8.5 Subroutine Flow Chart 47
      8.6 Subroutine Descriptions 47
      8.7 Sample Output 51

9.0   Program STABQ (Calculates atmospheric stability statistics) 60
      9.1 Description of Program 60
      9.2 Input Cards 60
      9.3 Discussion of Output 60
      9.4 Implementation 60
      9.5 Subroutine Flow Chart 60
      9.6 Subroutine Descriptions 60
      9.7 Sample Output 62

10.0 Program TDP (Calculate temperature and dew point statistics) ... 67
      10.1 Description of Program 67
      10.2 Input Cards 67
      10.3 Discussion of Output 67
      10.4 Implementation 67
      10.5 Subroutine Flow Chart 68
      10.6 Subroutine Descriptions 68
      10.7 Sample Output 70

APPENDIX A   NRC Standard Format for Meteorological Data

APPENDIX B   Program Listing of DATE

APPENDIX C   Program Listing of JFREQ

APPENDIX D   Program Listing of MISS

APPENDIX E   Program Listing of PRECP

APPENDIX F   Program Listing of PRINT

APPENDIX G   Program Listing of QA

APPENDIX H   Program Listing of STABQ

APPENDIX I   Program Listing TDP

1.0 INTRODUCTION

Regulatory Guide 1.70, Revision 2, "Standard Format and Content of Safety Analysis Reports for Nuclear Power Plants" (September 1975), recommended that, if possible, hour-by-hour meteorological data should be provided to the Nuclear Regulatory Commission (NRC) on magnetic tape. The purpose for this submission was to increase the NRC meteorology staff's ability to independently evaluate the environmental and safety related consequences of routine and accidental releases at nuclear power facilities. To avoid confusion and delays by the staff in the interpretation of meterological data submitted, a letter was sent on April 22, 1977 to all power reactor licensees and applicants with applications for a license to operate or construct a power reactor. This letter contained the details of a standardized format for submittal of hourly meteorological data on magnetic tape to the NRC. Subsequent to this letter, the NRC meteorology staff developed a number of computer programs to review and utilize the meteorological data submitted in this Standard Format. These programs are routinely used by the staff to examine and assess the quality of the data submitted as well as to convert the data to formats that are compatible as input to other NRC computer programs.

Programs DATE, MISS, PRINT, QA and STABQ are used to examine the quality and validity of the applicant's hourly meteorological data. Program JFREQ is used to calculate a joint frequency distribution of wind speed, wind direction and atmospheric stability that can be used in the NRC meteorological computer programs XOQDOQ (based on R.G. 1.111) and PAVAN (based on R.G. 1.145) for routine and accidental release meteorological analyses, respectively. These analyses, in turn, are used to assure that the radiological consequences of normal operation meet the As Low As Reasonably Achievable guidelines of 10 CFR 50, Appendix I, and that the radiological consequences of accidents conform to the provisions of 10 CFR 100, 10 CFR 51, and the Statement of Interim Policy on Nuclear Power Plant Accident Considerations Under the National Environmental Policy Act of 1969@ 45 FR 40101. Program PRECP is used to assess the quality of the applicants precipitation data prior to its use in the NRC CRAC computer code, a code which is used to assess the accident risk associated with the operation of nuclear power facilities. Program TDP is used to provide meteorological information to the hydrologic engineers to aid in their ultimate heat sink analysis.

A complete description of each of these programs is provided in this NUREG. Included with each code is a description of what it does, the input requirements to run it, a description of each subroutine, sample output and a listing of each program.

These programs were developed on an IBM 370 computer system in the FORTRAN IV language and should convert easily to other systems.

2.0 BACKGROUND

The purpose of standarizing the format for meteorological data* submitted to the NRC was to minimize the staff time necessary to utilize and interpret this data. If each applicant were to submit data in their own format, an inordinate amount of time could have been spent in trying to process the data. However, because each site had a different meteorological program, the format had to be flexible enough to handle any differences from one site to another. The result was a format that could handle almost all meteorological parameters anticipated to be recorded at a nuclear power facility. The only major drawback of the format was that it used up a large amount of space due to the many empty data fields where no information was available.

The diversity of the data available from site to site also led to additional programming considerations. In writing the programs to process the data, the intent was to keep them as simple as possible so they would be easily adaptable to other computer systems. However, a minimum amount of complexity was needed to address the differences in data available at each site and handle blank data fields. It was also necessary to have a consistent interpretation of the data between each of the programs.

2.1 Blank Data Fields

According to the criteria for the Standard Format (see Appendix A), if a specific meteorological parameter is not available for the entire data set, the appropriate field for that parameter may be left blank. To avoid confusion with computer systems that interpret a blank field as a value of zero, each program checks for blank fields. If they are found they are converted to the appropriate code for missing data.

2.2 Erroneous Data

Except for the programs DATE (which only reads the dates) and PRINT (which is used to list all the data as it is), each of the codes has a built in limit beyond which the data are considered as erroneous. These limits are consistent for all the programs and are as follows.

parameter	lower limit	upper limit	units
wind direction	0.0	365.0	degrees
wind speed	0.0	99.9	meters/second
sigma theta	0.0	365.0	degrees
temperature	-99.9	99.9	degrees C
dew point	-99.9	100.0	degrees C
delta-T	-7.0	35.0	degrees C/100 meters
precipitation	0.0	254.0	mm/hour

---

*
See Appendix A for the NRC Standard Format for Meteorological Data.

3.0 DATE

3.1 Description of Program

Date reviews a data set in the NRC Standard Format for the correct sequential ordering of the data by year, Julian day and hour.

3.2 Input Cards

Card	Column	Format	Variable	Description
1	1	I1	LL	Coding of hourly data: LL=0, coded 0000-2300 LL=1, coded 0100-2400
	2	1x		Blank
	3-74	18A4	Title	Title for output

3.3 Discussion of Output

The output consists of the date of the first data record that is read, the dates and record number of any data that is found to be out-of-sequence for any reason, and the date of the last data record that is read. When an error in the data sequence is found, the two sequential records where the error occurs will be listed.

3.4 Implementation

Input Units
     1 - data file of hourly meteorological data in NRC Standard Format
     5 - input card 1

Output Unit
     - defaults to printer

3.5 Subroutine Flow Chart

This program contains no subroutines.

3.6 Subroutine Description

This program contains no subroutines.

3.7 Sample Output

PROGRAM: DATE   VERSION: 1   DATED: MARCH 1982   RUN DATE: THURSDAY   MAY 13, 1982

SITE:

    TEST DATA

CONTAINS DATA FROM DECEMBER 1980 TO JANUARY 1981

BAD DATA DATES INSERTED TO CHECK PROGRAM DATE

HOURLY DATA CODED 0100 TO 2400

TITLE: SAMPLE RUN : INPUT FILE = DATA2   (SEE SAMPLE OUTPUT FOR PROGRAM PRINT)

HOURLY DATA CODED: 01-24

PROGRAM: DATE   VERSION: 1   DATED: MARCH 1982

SAMPLE RUN: INPUT FILE = DATA2   (SEE SAMPLE OUTPUT FOR PROGRAM PRINT)

DATE OF FIRST DATA RECORD READ: 80 365 12

BAD DATE SEQUENCE IN DATA: 80 365 15   RECORD   4
                            80   0   0   RECORD   5

BAD DATE SEQUENCE IN DATA: 80   0   0   RECORD   5
                            80 365 17   RECORD   6

BAD DATE SEQUENCE IN DATA: 80 365 20   RECORD   9
                            80 345 11   RECORD 10

BAD DATE SEQUENCE IN DATA: 80 345 11   RECORD 10
                            80 365 22   RECORD 11

BAD DATE SEQUENCE IN DATA: 80 365   RECORD 14
                            82 366   2   RECORD 15

BAD DATE SEQUENCE IN DATA: 82 366   2   RECORD 15
                            80 366   3   RECORD 16

BAD DATE SEQUENCE IN DATA: 80 345 11   RECORD 24
                            80 366 11   RECORD 25

BAD DATE SEQUENCE IN DATA: 80 366 11   RECORD 25
                            80 366 13   RECORD 26

BAD DATE SEQUENCE IN DATA: 81   1   1   RECORD 38
                            81   4   2   RECORD 39

BAD DATE SEQUENCE IN DATA: 81   4   2   RECORD 39
                            81   1   3   RECORD 40

BAD DATE SEQUENCE IN DATA: 81   1 19   RECORD 56
                            99 999 99   RECORD 57

BAD DATE SEQUENCE IN DATA: 99 999 99   RECORD 57
                            81   1 21   RECORD 58

BAD DATE SEQUENCE IN DATA: 81   2   3   RECORD 64
                            81   2   8   RECORD 65

BAD DATE SEQUENCE IN DATA: 81   2   8   RECORD 65
                            81   2   5   RECORD 66

6

PROGRAM: DATE   VERSION: 1   DATED: MARCH 1982   RUN DATE: THURSDAY   MAY 13, 1982

SAMPLE RUN : INPUT FILE = DATA2   (SEE SAMPLE OUTPUT FOR PROGRAM PRINT)

DATE OF LAST DATA RECORD READ: 81   2 11   RECORD NO.   72

4.0 JFREQ

4.1 Description of Program

JFREQ derives a joint frequency distribution of wind speed, wind direction and atmospheric stability from meteorological data in the NRC Standard Format. Atmospheric stability can be determined using either a vertical temperature gradient (in degrees C per 100 meters) or sigma theta. The distribution is printed in both hours and percent along with various summarizations of the data. The option of having the hourly data punched on cards is also available.

4.2 Input Cards

Card	Column	Format	Variable	Description
1	1-72	18A4	A	Title to be printed on each page of the output.
2	1	I1	ILEV	Level of wind data to be used. ILEV=1, Upper (U). ILEV=2, Intermediate (I). ILEV=3, Lower (L).
	2	I1	IS	Delta T interval to be used. IS=1, U-L IS=2, U-I IS=3, I-L Sigma theta level to be used. IS=4, Upper IS=5, Intermediate IS=6, Lower
	3	I1	IP	Option to punch the hourly joint frequency distribution. IP=0, do not punch IP=1, punch
	4	I1	LSH	Coding of hourly data. LSH=0, 0000-2300 hours LSH=1, 0100-2400 hours
	5	I1	IPS	Print hourly stability class by hour of day. IPS=0, do not print IPS=1, print
	6-10	F5.2	CALM	Wind speed that defines calm winds (must be >0.0 and <0.5 m/s)
	11-17	F7.1	VB	Code for variable wind direction. VB=0.0 if there are no variable wind directions.

Card	Column	Format	Variable	Description
3	1-6	3I2	IY(1) IM(1) ID(1)	The year, month and day that calculations are to begin.
	7	1x		Blank.
	8-13	3I2	IY(2) IM(2) ID(2)	The year, month and day that calculations are to end.

4.3 Discussion of Output

The output is divided into three sections. The first section lists the stability class by hour of day. The second section gives the joint frequency distribution in hours and the third section gives the joint frequency distribution in percent. All percentages in the third section are based on the total number of hours shown at the end of the hourly summaries in the second section. The number of hours (or percent) of variable winds and calm winds in each stability category is included in the total number of hours (or percent) shown for that stability. In addition, the variable winds are summarized separately at the end of each of the joint frequency distributions. Punched output will contain the hourly data in the same order as the printout shows it, except for the first card which will contain the hours of calm, and the variable winds which will not be punched. The format is as follows:

    Card 1-4:   Description cards
    Card 5:   7I5 (calms for stability A, B, ..., G)
    Card 6-75: 16I5 (hourly data for 7 stability classes with 10 wind
                categories per stability class)

The appropriate titles and total number of hours are punched out to aid in identification of the card output.

4.4 Implementation

If more than one joint frequency distribution is desired from the same data file, it may be obtained by inserting as many input cards 1, 2, and 3 as desired, as long as the dates specified are chronological. That is the program that will not go back and reread records from the data file that have already been read.

Input Units

    1 - data file of hourly meteorological data
    5 - input cards 1, 2, and 3

Output Unit

    6 - printer

4.5 Subroutine Flow Chart

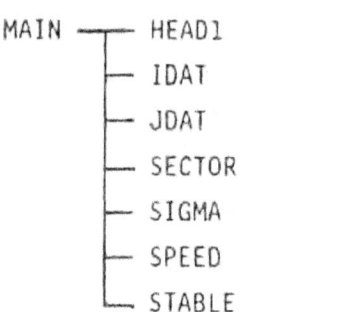

```
MAIN ──┬── HEAD1
       ├── IDAT
       ├── JDAT
       ├── SECTOR
       ├── SIGMA
       ├── SPEED
       └── STABLE
```

4.6 Subroutine Descriptions

Except for MAIN, all subroutines are listed alphabetically.

MAIN

The main part of the program initializes all data, reads the input cards, reads the data file, summarizes all data into the joint frequency distribution, calls all the subroutines, prints out all the results, and punches output if required.

HEAD1

This routine prints out the input parameters that were specified.

IDAT

This routine converts a given month and day to an equivalent Julian day.

JDAT

This routine converts a given Julian day to an equivalent month and day.

SECTOR

This routine distributes the wind direction data into 16 sectors centered on the principle compass points using the following equation.

SECTOR = 1+[(DIR+11.25)/22.5]

if SECTOR = 17, change to SECTOR = 1

where SECTOR = direction sector wind is blowing from
            (SECTOR should be truncated to nearest whole number)
      DIR = direction wind is blowing from (degrees)

Wind directions that coincide with a CALM wind speed are placed into sector 17. Wind directions that are considered variable are placed into sector 18.

SIGMA

This routine computes stability class from the horizontal deviation of wind direction (sigma theta) as follows.

Sigma theta (degrees)	Category	Stability Class
$22.5 \leq \sigma\theta$	1	A
$17.5 \leq \sigma\theta < 22.5$	2	B
$12.5 \leq \sigma\theta < 17.5$	3	C
$7.5 \leq \sigma\theta < 12.5$	4	D
$3.8 \leq \sigma\theta < 7.5$	5	E
$2.1 \leq \sigma\theta < 3.8$	6	F
$\sigma\theta < 2.1$	7	G

SPEED

This routine distributes the wind speed data into 10 different categories in meters per second as follows.

Wind speed (m/s)	Category
CALM	1
$CALM < U \leq 0.50$	2
$0.50 < U \leq 0.75$	3
$0.75 < U \leq 1.00$	4
$1.00 < U \leq 1.50$	5
$1.50 < U \leq 2.00$	6
$2.00 < U \leq 3.00$	7
$3.00 < U \leq 5.00$	8
$5.00 < U \leq 10.00$	9
$10.00 < U$	10

The variable CALM on input card 2 must be a wind speed greater than 0.0 and less than 0.5 m/s.

STABLE

This routine computes the stability class from atmospheric temperature gradient (delta-T) as follows.

Delta-T (°C/100m)	Category	Stability Class
$\Delta T \leq -1.9$	1	A
$-1.9 < \Delta T \leq -1.7$	2	B
$-1.7 < \Delta T \leq -1.5$	3	C
$-1.5 < \Delta T \leq -0.5$	4	D
$-0.5 < \Delta T \leq 1.5$	5	E
$1.5 < \Delta T \leq 4.0$	6	F
$4.0 < \Delta T$	7	G

4.7 Sample Output

PROGRAM: JFREQ   VERSION: 3   DATED: FEBRUARY 1982   RUN DATE: FRIDAY   MAY 7, 1982

TITLE: SAMPLE RUN : INPUT FILE = DATA1 (SEE SAMPLE OUTPUT FOR PROGRAM PRINT)

WIND DATA FROM LEVEL: LOWER

DELTA-T INTERVAL: INTERMEDIATE MINUS   LOWER

PUNCH HOURLY JFD ON CARDS: NO

HOURLY DATA CODED: 01-24

WRITE STABILITY CLASS BY HOUR OF DAY: YES

CALM WINDS CODED: 0 27 M/S

VARIABLE WIND DIRECTION CODED: 8888.8

JFD FOR DATA PERIOD: BEGINING - 80 12 30
                        ENDING   - 81 1 3

13

PROGRAM: JFREQ   VERSION: 3   DATED: FEBRUARY 1982   RUN DATE: FRIDAY   MAY 7, 1982

SITE: TEST DATA

CONTAINS DATA FROM DECEMBER 1980 TO JANUARY 1891

HOURLY DATA CODED 0100 TO 2400

****

SAMPLE RUN : INPUT FILE = DATA1   (SEE SAMPLE OUTPUT FOR PROGRAM PRINT)

LEVEL OF WIND DATA: 10.0 METERS   DELTA T LAYER: 60.0 - 10.0 METERS

STABILITY CLASS BY HOUR OF DAY

													HOUR											
YR	MN	DY	1	2	3	4	5	6	7	8	9	10	11	12	13	14	15	16	17	18	19	20	21	22	23	24
80	12	30	-	-	-	-	I	I	I	I	I	-	I	E	E	E	E	D	D	D	C	C	C	C	C	C
80	12	31	B	B	C	A	A	D	D	D	E	E	E	E	E	D	D	D	D	C	I	C	I	C	C	F
81	1	1	B	B	C	F	G	D	D	A	-	E	E	E	E	D	D	D	-	C	C	C	C	C	C	C

15

PROGRAM: JFREQ   VERSION: 3   DATED: FEBRUARY 1982   RUN DATE: FRIDAY   MAY 7, 1982

SAMPLE RUN : INPUT FILE = DATA1 (SEE SAMPLE OUTPUT FOR PROGRAM PRINT)

LEVEL OF WIND DATA: 10.0 METERS   DELTA T LAYER: 60.0 - 10.0 METERS

JOINT FREQUENCY DISTRIBUTION OF WIND SPEED AND DIRECTION IN HOURS   ATMOSPHERIC STABILITY CLASS A

U (M/S)	N	NNE	NE	ENE	E	ESE	SE	SSE	S	SSW	SW	WSW	W	WNW	NW	NNW	TOTAL
CALM	0	0	0	0	0	0	0	0	0	0	0	0	0	0	0	0	0
.5-.75	0	0	0	0	0	0	0	0	0	0	0	0	0	0	0	0	0
.75-1.0	0	0	0	0	0	0	0	0	0	0	0	0	0	0	0	0	0
1.0-1.5	0	0	0	0	0	0	0	0	0	0	0	0	0	0	0	0	0
1.5-2.0	0	0	0	0	0	0	0	0	0	0	0	0	0	0	0	0	0
2.0-3.0	0	0	0	0	0	0	0	0	0	0	0	0	0	0	0	0	0
3.0-5.0	0	0	0	0	0	0	0	0	0	0	0	0	0	0	0	0	0
5.0-10.0	0	0	0	0	0	0	0	0	0	0	0	0	0	0	0	0	0
>10.0	0	0	0	0	0	0	0	0	0	0	0	0	0	0	0	0	0
VARIABLE																	
TOTAL	0	0	0	0	0	0	0	0	0	0	0	0	0	0	0	0	0

JOINT FREQUENCY DISTRIBUTION OF WIND SPEED AND DIRECTION IN HOURS   ATMOSPHERIC STABILITY CLASS B

U (M/S)	N	NNE	NE	ENE	E	ESE	SE	SSE	S	SSW	SW	WSW	W	WNW	NW	NNW	TOTAL
CALM	0	0	0	0	0	0	0	0	0	0	0	0	0	0	0	0	0
.5-.75	0	0	0	0	0	0	0	0	0	0	0	0	0	0	0	0	0
.75-1.0	0	0	0	0	0	0	0	0	0	0	0	0	0	0	0	0	0
1.0-1.5	0	2	2	0	0	0	0	0	0	0	0	0	0	1	1	0	6
1.5-2.0	0	0	0	0	0	0	0	0	0	0	0	0	0	0	0	0	0
2.0-3.0	0	0	0	0	0	0	0	0	0	0	0	0	0	0	0	0	0
3.0-5.0	0	0	0	0	0	0	0	0	0	0	0	0	0	0	0	0	0
5.0-10.0	0	0	0	0	0	0	0	0	0	0	0	0	0	0	0	0	0
>10.0	0	0	0	0	0	0	0	0	0	0	0	0	0	0	0	0	0
VARIABLE																	
TOTAL	0	2	2	0	0	0	0	0	0	0	0	0	0	1	1	0	6

JOINT FREQUENCY DISTRIBUTION OF WIND SPEED AND DIRECTION IN HOURS   ATMOSPHERIC STABILITY CLASS C

U (M/S)	N	NNE	NE	ENE	E	ESE	SE	SSE	S	SSW	SW	WSW	W	WNW	NW	NNW	TOTAL
CALM	0	0	0	0	0	0	0	0	0	0	0	0	0	0	0	0	0
.5-.75	0	0	0	0	0	0	0	0	0	0	0	0	0	0	0	0	0
.75-1.0	0	2	0	0	0	0	0	0	0	0	0	1	0	0	0	0	3
1.0-1.5	0	0	2	0	0	0	0	0	0	0	0	0	0	0	0	0	2
1.5-2.0	0	0	0	2	0	0	0	0	0	0	0	0	0	0	0	1	3
2.0-3.0	0	0	0	2	0	0	0	0	0	0	0	0	0	0	0	0	2
3.0-5.0	0	0	0	0	2	0	0	0	0	0	0	0	0	0	0	0	2
5.0-10.0	0	0	0	0	4	0	0	0	1	0	0	0	0	0	0	0	5
>10.0	0	0	0	0	0	0	0	0	0	0	0	0	0	0	0	0	0
VARIABLE																	
TOTAL	0	2	2	4	6	0	0	0	1	0	0	1	0	0	0	1	17

CALM= 0.27 M/S

PROGRAM: JFREQ   VERSION: 3   DATED: FEBRUARY 1982

RUN DATE: FRIDAY   MAY 7, 1982

SAMPLE RUN : INPUT FILE = DATA1 (SEE SAMPLE OUTPUT FOR PROGRAM PRINT)

LEVEL OF WIND DATA: 10.0 METERS   DELTA T LAYER: 60.0- 10.0 METERS

JOINT FREQUENCY DISTRIBUTION OF WIND SPEED AND DIRECTION IN HOURS   ATMOSPHERIC STABILITY CLASS D

U (M/S)	N	NNE	NE	ENE	E	ESE	SE	SSE	S	SSW	SW	WSW	W	WNW	NW	NNW	TOTAL
CALM-.5	0	0	0	0	0	0	0	0	0	0	0	0	0	0	0	0	0
.5-.75	0	0	0	0	0	0	0	0	0	0	0	0	0	0	0	0	0
.75-1.0	0	0	0	0	0	0	0	0	0	0	0	0	0	0	0	0	0
1.0-1.5	0	0	0	0	0	0	0	0	0	0	0	0	0	0	0	0	0
1.5-2.0	0	0	0	0	0	0	0	0	0	0	0	0	0	0	0	0	0
2.0-3.0	0	0	0	0	0	0	0	0	0	0	0	0	0	0	0	0	0
3.0-5.0	0	0	0	0	0	0	0	0	0	0	0	0	0	0	0	0	0
5.0-10.0	0	0	0	0	4	0	0	0	0	0	0	0	0	0	0	0	4
>10.0	0	0	0	0	0	0	0	0	0	0	0	0	0	0	0	0	0
VARIABLE	0	0	0	0	0	0	0	0	0	0	0	0	0	0	0	0	0
TOTAL	0	0	0	0	4	0	0	0	0	0	0	0	0	0	0	0	4

JOINT FREQUENCY DISTRIBUTION OF WIND SPEED AND DIRECTION IN HOURS   ATMOSPHERIC STABILITY CLASS E

U (M/S)	N	NNE	NE	ENE	E	ESE	SE	SSE	S	SSW	SW	WSW	W	WNW	NW	NNW	TOTAL
CALM-.5	0	0	0	0	0	0	0	0	0	0	0	0	0	0	0	0	0
.5-.75	0	0	0	0	0	0	0	0	0	0	0	0	0	0	0	0	0
.75-1.0	0	0	0	0	0	0	1	0	2	0	0	0	0	0	0	0	3
1.0-1.5	0	0	0	0	0	0	0	0	0	0	0	0	0	0	0	0	0
1.5-2.0	0	0	0	0	0	0	0	0	0	0	0	0	0	0	0	0	0
2.0-3.0	0	0	0	0	0	0	0	0	0	0	0	0	0	0	0	0	0
3.0-5.0	0	0	0	0	1	0	0	0	0	0	0	0	0	0	0	0	1
5.0-10.0	0	1	0	0	0	0	0	0	0	0	0	0	0	0	0	0	1
>10.0	0	0	0	0	0	0	0	0	0	0	0	0	0	0	0	0	0
VARIABLE	1	0	0	0	0	0	0	0	0	0	0	0	0	0	0	0	1
TOTAL	1	1	0	0	5	0	0	1	2	0	0	0	0	0	0	0	12

JOINT FREQUENCY DISTRIBUTION OF WIND SPEED AND DIRECTION IN HOURS   ATMOSPHERIC STABILITY CLASS F

U (M/S)	N	NNE	NE	ENE	E	ESE	SE	SSE	S	SSW	SW	WSW	W	WNW	NW	NNW	TOTAL
CALM-.5	0	0	0	0	0	0	0	0	0	0	0	0	0	0	0	0	0
.5-.75	0	0	0	0	0	0	0	0	0	0	0	0	0	0	0	0	0
.75-1.0	0	0	0	0	0	0	0	0	0	0	0	0	0	0	0	0	0
1.0-1.5	0	0	0	0	0	0	0	0	0	0	0	0	0	0	0	0	0
1.5-2.0	0	0	0	0	0	0	0	0	0	0	0	0	0	1	0	0	1
2.0-3.0	0	0	0	0	0	0	0	0	0	0	0	0	0	0	0	0	0
3.0-5.0	0	0	0	0	0	0	0	0	0	0	0	0	0	0	0	0	0
5.0-10.0	0	0	0	0	0	0	0	0	0	0	0	0	0	0	0	0	0
>10.0	0	0	0	0	0	0	0	0	0	0	0	0	0	0	0	0	0
VARIABLE	0	0	0	0	0	0	0	0	0	0	0	0	0	0	0	0	0
TOTAL	0	0	0	0	0	0	0	0	0	0	0	0	1	0	0	0	1

CALM= 0.27 M/S

17

SAMPLE RUN : INPUT FILE = DATA1   (SEE SAMPLE OUTPUT FOR PROGRAM PRINT)

LEVEL OF WIND DATA: 10.0 METERS   DELTA T LAYER: 60.0 - 10.0 METERS

JOINT FREQUENCY DISTRIBUTION OF WIND SPEED AND DIRECTION IN HOURS   ATMOSPHERIC STABILITY CLASS G.

U (M/S)	N	NNE	NE	ENE	E	ESE	SE	SSE	S	SSW	SW	WSW	W	WNW	NW	NNW	TOTAL
CALM																	
.5-.75	0	0	0	0	0	0	0	0	0	0	0	0	0	0	0	0	0
.75-1.0	0	0	0	0	0	0	0	0	0	0	0	0	0	0	0	0	0
1.0-1.5	0	0	0	0	0	0	0	0	0	0	0	0	0	0	0	0	0
1.5-2.0	0	0	0	0	0	0	0	0	0	0	0	0	0	0	0	0	0
2.0-3.0	0	0	0	0	0	0	0	0	0	0	0	0	0	0	0	0	0
3.0-5.0	0	0	0	0	0	0	0	0	0	0	0	0	0	0	0	0	0
5.0-10.0	0	0	0	0	0	0	0	0	0	0	0	0	0	0	0	0	0
>10.0	0	0	0	0	0	0	0	0	0	0	0	0	0	0	0	0	0
VARIABLE	0	0	0	0	0	0	0	0	0	0	0	0	0	0	0	0	0
TOTAL	0	0	0	0	0	0	0	0	0	0	0	0	0	0	0	0	0

JOINT FREQUENCY DISTRIBUTION OF WIND SPEED AND DIRECTION IN HOURS   ATMOSPHERIC STABILITY CLASS ALL

U (M/S)	N	NNE	NE	ENE	E	ESE	SE	SSE	S	SSW	SW	WSW	W	WNW	NW	NNW	TOTAL
CALM																	
.5-.75	0	0	0	0	0	0	0	0	0	0	0	0	0	0	0	0	0
.75-1.0	0	2	0	0	0	0	0	1	2	0	0	0	0	0	0	0	6
1.0-1.5	0	2	4	0	0	0	0	0	0	0	0	1	1	1	1	1	9
1.5-2.0	0	0	0	2	0	0	0	3	0	0	0	0	0	0	0	0	3
2.0-3.0	0	0	0	2	0	0	0	0	0	0	0	0	0	0	0	0	2
3.0-5.0	1	0	0	0	0	0	0	0	0	0	0	0	0	0	0	0	8
5.0-10.0	0	1	0	0	6	0	0	0	0	0	0	0	0	0	0	0	10
>10.0					9				1								2
VARIABLE	1												1			1	
TOTAL	1	5	6	6	15	0	0	1	3	0	1	1	1	1	1	1	40

CALM= 0.27 M/S

TOTAL VALID HOURS =   40   TOTAL POSSIBLE HOURS =   72

OVERALL STABILITY CLASS FREQUENCIES IN HOURS

STABILITY:	A	B	C	D	E	F	G	ALL
FREQUENCY:	0	6	17	4	12	1	0	40

OVERALL WIND SPEED FREQUENCIES IN HOURS

WIND SPEED (M/S):	CALM	.5-.75	.75-1.0	1.0-1.5	1.5-2.0	2.0-3.0	3.0-5.0	5.0-10.0	>10.0	VARIABLE
FREQUENCY:	0	0	6	2	3	18	2	8	10	2
CUMULATIVE FREQ:	0	0	6	15	15	18	20	23	38	2

PROGRAM: JFREQ   VERSION: 3   DATED: FEBRUARY 1982   RUN DATE: FRIDAY   MAY ., 1982

SAMPLE RUN : INPUT FILE = DATA1   (SEE SAMPLE OUTPUT FOR PROGRAM PRINT)

LEVEL OF WIND DATA: 10.0 METERS   DELTA T LAYER: 60.0- 10.0 METERS

DISTRIBUTION OF VARIABLE WINDS

U (M/S)	A	B	C	D	E	F	G	TOTAL
CALM-.5	0	0	0	0	0	0	0	0
.5-.75	0	0	0	0	0	0	0	0
.75-1.0	0	0	0	0	0	0	0	0
1.0-1.5	0	0	0	0	0	0	0	0
1.5-2.0	0	0	0	0	0	0	0	0
2.0-3.0	0	0	0	0	0	0	0	0
3.0-5.0	0	0	0	0	0	0	0	0
5.0-10.0	0	0	0	0	2	0	0	2
>10.0	0	0	0	0	0	0	0	0
TOTAL	0	0	0	0	2	0	0	2

PROGRAM: JFREQ   VERSION: 3   DATED: FEBRUARY 1982   RUN DATE: FRIDAY   MAY 7, 1982

SAMPLE RUN : INPUT FILE = DATA1   (SEE SAMPLE OUTPUT FOR PROGRAM PRINT)

LEVEL OF WIND DATA: 10.0 METERS   DELTA T LAYER: 60.0- 10.0 METERS

JOINT FREQUENCY DISTRIBUTION OF WIND SPEED AND DIRECTION IN FRACTIONS   ATMOSPHERIC STABILITY CLASS A

U (M/S)	N	NNE	NE	ENE	E	ESE	SE	SSE	S	SSW	SW	WSW	W	WNW	NW	NNW	TOTAL
CALM	0.0	0.0	0.0	0.0	0.0	0.0	0.0	0.0	0.0	0.0	0.0	0.0	0.0	0.0	0.0	0.0	0.0
CALM-.5	0.0	0.0	0.0	0.0	0.0	0.0	0.0	0.0	0.0	0.0	0.0	0.0	0.0	0.0	0.0	0.0	0.0
.5-.75	0.0	0.0	0.0	0.0	0.0	0.0	0.0	0.0	0.0	0.0	0.0	0.0	0.0	0.0	0.0	0.0	0.0
.75-1.0	0.0	0.0	0.0	0.0	0.0	0.0	0.0	0.0	0.0	0.0	0.0	0.0	0.0	0.0	0.0	0.0	0.0
1.0-1.5	0.0	0.0	0.0	0.0	0.0	0.0	0.0	0.0	0.0	0.0	0.0	0.0	0.0	0.0	0.0	0.0	0.0
1.5-2.0	0.0	0.0	0.0	0.0	0.0	0.0	0.0	0.0	0.0	0.0	0.0	0.0	0.0	0.0	0.0	0.0	0.0
2.0-3.0	0.0	0.0	0.0	0.0	0.0	0.0	0.0	0.0	0.0	0.0	0.0	0.0	0.0	0.0	0.0	0.0	0.0
3.0-5.0	0.0	0.0	0.0	0.0	0.0	0.0	0.0	0.0	0.0	0.0	0.0	0.0	0.0	0.0	0.0	0.0	0.0
5.0-10.0	0.0	0.0	0.0	0.0	0.0	0.0	0.0	0.0	0.0	0.0	0.0	0.0	0.0	0.0	0.0	0.0	0.0
>10.0	0.0	0.0	0.0	0.0	0.0	0.0	0.0	0.0	0.0	0.0	0.0	0.0	0.0	0.0	0.0	0.0	0.0
VARIABLE	0.0	0.0	0.0	0.0	0.0	0.0	0.0	0.0	0.0	0.0	0.0	0.0	0.0	0.0	0.0	0.0	0.0
TOTAL	0.0	0.0	0.0	0.0	0.0	0.0	0.0	0.0	0.0	0.0	0.0	0.0	0.0	0.0	0.0	0.0	0.0

JOINT FREQUENCY DISTRIBUTION OF WIND SPEED AND DIRECTION IN FRACTIONS   ATMOSPHERIC STABILITY CLASS B

U (M/S)	N	NNE	NE	ENE	E	ESE	SE	SSE	S	SSW	SW	WSW	W	WNW	NW	NNW	TOTAL
CALM	0.0	0.0	0.0	0.0	0.0	0.0	0.0	0.0	0.0	0.0	0.0	0.0	0.0	0.0	0.0	0.0	0.0
CALM-.5	0.0	0.0	0.0	0.0	0.0	0.0	0.0	0.0	0.0	0.0	0.0	0.0	0.0	0.0	0.0	0.0	0.0
.5-.75	0.0	5.00	0.0	0.0	0.0	0.0	0.0	0.0	0.0	0.0	0.0	0.0	0.0	2.50	2.50	0.0	15.00
.75-1.0	0.0	0.0	5.00	0.0	0.0	0.0	0.0	0.0	0.0	0.0	0.0	0.0	0.0	2.50	0.0	0.0	0.0
1.0-1.5	0.0	0.0	0.0	0.0	0.0	0.0	0.0	0.0	0.0	0.0	0.0	0.0	0.0	0.0	0.0	0.0	0.0
1.5-2.0	0.0	0.0	0.0	0.0	0.0	0.0	0.0	0.0	0.0	0.0	0.0	0.0	0.0	0.0	0.0	0.0	0.0
2.0-3.0	0.0	0.0	0.0	0.0	0.0	0.0	0.0	0.0	0.0	0.0	0.0	0.0	0.0	0.0	0.0	0.0	0.0
3.0-5.0	0.0	0.0	0.0	0.0	0.0	0.0	0.0	0.0	0.0	0.0	0.0	0.0	0.0	0.0	0.0	0.0	0.0
5.0-10.0	0.0	0.0	0.0	0.0	0.0	0.0	0.0	0.0	0.0	0.0	0.0	0.0	0.0	0.0	0.0	0.0	0.0
>10.0	0.0	0.0	0.0	0.0	0.0	0.0	0.0	0.0	0.0	0.0	0.0	0.0	0.0	0.0	0.0	0.0	0.0
VARIABLE	0.0	0.0	0.0	0.0	0.0	0.0	0.0	0.0	0.0	0.0	0.0	0.0	0.0	0.0	0.0	0.0	0.0
TOTAL	0.0	5.00	5.00	10.00	0.0	0.0	0.0	0.0	0.0	0.0	0.0	0.0	0.0	2.50	2.50	0.0	15.00

JOINT FREQUENCY DISTRIBUTION OF WIND SPEED AND DIRECTION IN FRACTIONS   ATMOSPHERIC STABILITY CLASS C

U (M/S)	N	NNE	NE	ENE	E	ESE	SE	SSE	S	SSW	SW	WSW	W	WNW	NW	NNW	TOTAL
CALM	0.0	0.0	0.0	0.0	0.0	0.0	0.0	0.0	0.0	0.0	0.0	0.0	0.0	0.0	0.0	0.0	0.0
CALM-.5	0.0	0.0	0.0	0.0	0.0	0.0	0.0	0.0	0.0	0.0	0.0	0.0	0.0	0.0	0.0	0.0	0.0
.5-.75	0.0	5.00	0.0	0.0	0.0	0.0	0.0	0.0	0.0	0.0	0.0	0.0	0.0	0.0	0.0	2.50	7.50
.75-1.0	0.0	0.0	5.00	0.0	0.0	0.0	0.0	0.0	0.0	0.0	0.0	0.0	0.0	0.0	0.0	0.0	5.00
1.0-1.5	0.0	0.0	0.0	0.0	0.0	0.0	0.0	0.0	0.0	0.0	2.50	0.0	0.0	0.0	0.0	0.0	7.50
1.5-2.0	0.0	0.0	0.0	5.00	0.0	0.0	0.0	0.0	0.0	0.0	0.0	0.0	0.0	0.0	0.0	0.0	5.00
2.0-3.0	0.0	0.0	0.0	5.00	0.0	0.0	0.0	0.0	0.0	0.0	0.0	0.0	0.0	0.0	0.0	0.0	5.00
3.0-5.0	0.0	0.0	0.0	0.0	0.0	0.0	0.0	0.0	0.0	0.0	0.0	0.0	0.0	0.0	0.0	0.0	0.0
5.0-10.0	0.0	0.0	0.0	0.0	5.00	0.0	0.0	0.0	2.50	0.0	0.0	0.0	0.0	0.0	0.0	0.0	12.50
>10.0	0.0	0.0	0.0	0.0	0.0	0.0	0.0	0.0	0.0	0.0	0.0	0.0	0.0	0.0	0.0	0.0	0.0
VARIABLE	0.0	0.0	0.0	0.0	0.0	0.0	0.0	0.0	0.0	0.0	0.0	0.0	0.0	0.0	0.0	0.0	0.0
TOTAL	0.0	5.00	5.00	10.00	15.00	0.0	0.0	0.0	2.50	0.0	2.50	0.0	0.0	0.0	0.0	2.50	42.50

CALM= 0.27 M/S

PROGRAM: JFREQ   VERSION: 3   DATED: FEBRUARY 1982   RUN DATE: FRIDAY   MAY 7, 1982

SAMPLE RUN : INPUT FILE = DATA1   (SEE SAMPLE OUTPUT FOR PROGRAM PRINT)

LEVEL OF WIND DATA: 10.0 METERS   DELTA T LAYER: 60.0- 10.0 METERS

JOINT FREQUENCY DISTRIBUTION OF WIND SPEED AND DIRECTION IN FRACTIONS   ATMOSPHERIC STABILITY CLASS D

U (M/S)	N	NNE	NE	ENE	E	ESE	SE	SSE	S	SSW	SW	WSW	W	WNW	NW	NNW	TOTAL
CALM-.5	0.0	0.0	0.0	0.0	0.0	0.0	0.0	0.0	0.0	0.0	0.0	0.0	0.0	0.0	0.0	0.0	0.0
.5-.75	0.0	0.0	0.0	0.0	0.0	0.0	0.0	0.0	0.0	0.0	0.0	0.0	0.0	0.0	0.0	0.0	0.0
.75-1.0	0.0	0.0	0.0	0.0	0.0	0.0	0.0	0.0	0.0	0.0	0.0	0.0	0.0	0.0	0.0	0.0	0.0
1.0-1.5	0.0	0.0	0.0	0.0	0.0	0.0	0.0	0.0	0.0	0.0	0.0	0.0	0.0	0.0	0.0	0.0	0.0
1.5-2.0	0.0	0.0	0.0	0.0	0.0	0.0	0.0	0.0	0.0	0.0	0.0	0.0	0.0	0.0	0.0	0.0	0.0
2.0-3.0	0.0	0.0	0.0	0.0	0.0	0.0	0.0	0.0	0.0	0.0	0.0	0.0	0.0	0.0	0.0	0.0	0.0
3.0-5.0	0.0	0.0	0.0	0.0	0.0	0.0	0.0	0.0	0.0	0.0	0.0	0.0	0.0	0.0	0.0	0.0	0.0
5.0-10.0	0.0	0.0	0.0	0.0	10.00	0.0	0.0	0.0	0.0	0.0	0.0	0.0	0.0	0.0	0.0	0.0	10.00
>10.0	0.0	0.0	0.0	0.0	0.0	0.0	0.0	0.0	0.0	0.0	0.0	0.0	0.0	0.0	0.0	0.0	0.0
VARIABLE	0.0	0.0	0.0	0.0	0.0	0.0	0.0	0.0	0.0	0.0	0.0	0.0	0.0	0.0	0.0	0.0	0.0
TOTAL	0.0	0.0	0.0	0.0	10.00	0.0	0.0	0.0	0.0	0.0	0.0	0.0	0.0	0.0	0.0	0.0	10.00

JOINT FREQUENCY DISTRIBUTION OF WIND SPEED AND DIRECTION IN FRACTIONS   ATMOSPHERIC STABILITY CLASS E

U (M/S)	N	NNE	NE	ENE	E	ESE	SE	SSE	S	SSW	SW	WSW	W	WNW	NW	NNW	TOTAL
CALM-.5	0.0	0.0	0.0	0.0	0.0	0.0	0.0	0.0	0.0	0.0	0.0	0.0	0.0	0.0	0.0	0.0	0.0
.5-.75	0.0	0.0	0.0	0.0	0.0	0.0	0.0	0.0	0.0	0.0	0.0	0.0	0.0	0.0	0.0	0.0	0.0
.75-1.0	0.0	0.0	0.0	0.0	0.0	0.0	0.0	0.0	0.0	0.0	0.0	0.0	0.0	0.0	0.0	0.0	0.0
1.0-1.5	0.0	0.0	0.0	0.0	0.0	0.0	0.0	2.50	5.00	0.0	0.0	0.0	0.0	0.0	0.0	0.0	7.50
1.5-2.0	0.0	0.0	0.0	0.0	0.0	0.0	0.0	0.0	0.0	0.0	0.0	0.0	0.0	0.0	0.0	0.0	0.0
2.0-3.0	0.0	0.0	0.0	0.0	0.0	0.0	0.0	0.0	0.0	0.0	0.0	0.0	0.0	0.0	0.0	0.0	0.0
3.0-5.0	0.0	0.0	0.0	0.0	0.0	0.0	0.0	0.0	0.0	0.0	0.0	0.0	0.0	0.0	0.0	0.0	0.0
5.0-10.0	2.50	2.50	0.0	0.0	10.00	0.0	0.0	0.0	0.0	0.0	0.0	0.0	0.0	0.0	0.0	0.0	15.00
>10.0	0.0	0.0	0.0	0.0	2.50	0.0	0.0	0.0	0.0	0.0	0.0	0.0	0.0	0.0	0.0	0.0	2.50
VARIABLE	0.0	0.0	0.0	0.0	0.0	0.0	0.0	0.0	0.0	0.0	0.0	0.0	0.0	0.0	0.0	0.0	0.0
TOTAL	2.50	2.50	0.0	0.0	12.50	0.0	0.0	2.50	5.00	0.0	0.0	0.0	0.0	0.0	0.0	0.0	30.00

JOINT FREQUENCY DISTRIBUTION OF WIND SPEED AND DIRECTION IN FRACTIONS   ATMOSPHERIC STABILITY CLASS F

U (M/S)	N	NNE	NE	ENE	E	ESE	SE	SSE	S	SSW	SW	WSW	W	WNW	NW	NNW	TOTAL
CALM-.5	0.0	0.0	0.0	0.0	0.0	0.0	0.0	0.0	0.0	0.0	0.0	0.0	0.0	0.0	0.0	0.0	0.0
.5-.75	0.0	0.0	0.0	0.0	0.0	0.0	0.0	0.0	0.0	0.0	0.0	0.0	0.0	0.0	0.0	0.0	0.0
.75-1.0	0.0	0.0	0.0	0.0	0.0	0.0	0.0	0.0	0.0	0.0	0.0	0.0	0.0	0.0	0.0	0.0	0.0
1.0-1.5	0.0	0.0	0.0	0.0	0.0	0.0	0.0	0.0	0.0	0.0	0.0	2.50	0.0	0.0	0.0	0.0	2.50
1.5-2.0	0.0	0.0	0.0	0.0	0.0	0.0	0.0	0.0	0.0	0.0	0.0	0.0	0.0	0.0	0.0	0.0	0.0
2.0-3.0	0.0	0.0	0.0	0.0	0.0	0.0	0.0	0.0	0.0	0.0	0.0	0.0	0.0	0.0	0.0	0.0	0.0
3.0-5.0	0.0	0.0	0.0	0.0	0.0	0.0	0.0	0.0	0.0	0.0	0.0	0.0	0.0	0.0	0.0	0.0	0.0
5.0-10.0	0.0	0.0	0.0	0.0	0.0	0.0	0.0	0.0	0.0	0.0	0.0	0.0	0.0	0.0	0.0	0.0	0.0
>10.0	0.0	0.0	0.0	0.0	0.0	0.0	0.0	0.0	0.0	0.0	0.0	0.0	0.0	0.0	0.0	0.0	0.0
VARIABLE	0.0	0.0	0.0	0.0	0.0	0.0	0.0	0.0	0.0	0.0	0.0	0.0	0.0	0.0	0.0	0.0	0.0
TOTAL	0.0	0.0	0.0	0.0	0.0	0.0	0.0	0.0	0.0	0.0	0.0	2.50	0.0	0.0	0.0	0.0	2.50

CALM= 0.27 M/S

21

PROGRAM: JFREQ   VERSION: 3   DATED: FEBRUARY 1982   RUN DATE: FRIDAY   MAY 7, 1982

SAMPLE RUN : INPUT FILE = DATA1   (SEE SAMPLE OUTPUT FOR PROGRAM PRINT)

LEVEL OF WIND DATA: 10.0 METERS   DELTA T LAYER: 60.0- 10.0 METERS

JOINT FREQUENCY DISTRIBUTION OF WIND SPEED AND DIRECTION IN FRACTIONS   ATMOSPHERIC STABILITY CLASS G

U (M/S)	N	NNE	NE	ENE	E	ESE	SE	SSE	S	SSW	SW	WSW	W	WNW	NW	NNW	TOTAL
CALM																	
CALM-.5	0.0	0.0	0.0	0.0	0.0	0.0	0.0	0.0	0.0	0.0	0.0	0.0	0.0	0.0	0.0	0.0	0.0
.5-.75	0.0	0.0	0.0	0.0	0.0	0.0	0.0	0.0	0.0	0.0	0.0	0.0	0.0	0.0	0.0	0.0	0.0
.75-1.0	0.0	0.0	0.0	0.0	0.0	0.0	0.0	0.0	0.0	0.0	0.0	0.0	0.0	0.0	0.0	0.0	0.0
1.0-1.5	0.0	0.0	0.0	0.0	0.0	0.0	0.0	0.0	0.0	0.0	0.0	0.0	0.0	0.0	0.0	0.0	0.0
1.5-2.0	0.0	0.0	0.0	0.0	0.0	0.0	0.0	0.0	0.0	0.0	0.0	0.0	0.0	0.0	0.0	0.0	0.0
2.0-3.0	0.0	0.0	0.0	0.0	0.0	0.0	0.0	0.0	0.0	0.0	0.0	0.0	0.0	0.0	0.0	0.0	0.0
3.0-5.0	0.0	0.0	0.0	0.0	0.0	0.0	0.0	0.0	0.0	0.0	0.0	0.0	0.0	0.0	0.0	0.0	0.0
5.0-10.0	0.0	0.0	0.0	0.0	0.0	0.0	0.0	0.0	0.0	0.0	0.0	0.0	0.0	0.0	0.0	0.0	0.0
>10.0	0.0	0.0	0.0	0.0	0.0	0.0	0.0	0.0	0.0	0.0	0.0	0.0	0.0	0.0	0.0	0.0	0.0
VARIABLE	0.0	0.0	0.0	0.0	0.0	0.0	0.0	0.0	0.0	0.0	0.0	0.0	0.0	0.0	0.0	0.0	0.0
TOTAL	0.0	0.0	0.0	0.0	0.0	0.0	0.0	0.0	0.0	0.0	0.0	0.0	0.0	0.0	0.0	0.0	0.0

JOINT FREQUENCY DISTRIBUTION OF WIND SPEED AND DIRECTION IN FRACTIONS   ATMOSPHERIC STABILITY CLASS ALL

U (M/S)	N	NNE	NE	ENE	E	ESE	SE	SSE	S	SSW	SW	WSW	W	WNW	NW	NNW	TOTAL
CALM																	
CALM-.5	0.0	0.0	0.0	0.0	0.0	0.0	0.0	0.0	0.0	0.0	0.0	0.0	0.0	0.0	0.0	0.0	0.0
.5-.75	0.0	0.0	0.0	0.0	0.0	0.0	0.0	0.0	0.0	0.0	0.0	0.0	0.0	0.0	0.0	0.0	0.0
.75-1.0	0.0	5.00	0.0	0.0	0.0	0.0	0.0	0.0	5.00	0.0	0.0	0.0	2.50	0.0	0.0	2.50	15.00
1.0-1.5	0.0	5.00	10.00	0.0	0.0	0.0	0.0	2.50	0.0	0.0	0.0	0.0	0.0	2.50	2.50	0.0	22.50
1.5-2.0	0.0	0.0	0.0	5.00	0.0	0.0	0.0	0.0	0.0	0.0	0.0	0.0	0.0	0.0	0.0	0.0	7.50
2.0-3.0	0.0	0.0	0.0	5.00	0.0	0.0	0.0	0.0	0.0	0.0	0.0	2.50	0.0	0.0	0.0	0.0	5.00
3.0-5.0	0.0	0.0	0.0	0.0	15.00	0.0	0.0	0.0	0.0	0.0	0.0	0.0	0.0	0.0	0.0	0.0	5.00
5.0-10.0	2.50	2.50	0.0	0.0	22.50	0.0	0.0	0.0	0.0	0.0	0.0	0.0	0.0	0.0	0.0	0.0	20.00
>10.0	0.0	0.0	0.0	0.0	0.0	0.0	0.0	0.0	0.0	0.0	0.0	0.0	0.0	0.0	0.0	0.0	25.00
VARIABLE	0.0	0.0	0.0	0.0	0.0	0.0	0.0	0.0	2.50	0.0	0.0	0.0	0.0	0.0	0.0	0.0	5.00
TOTAL	2.50	12.50	10.00	10.00	37.50	0.0	0.0	2.50	7.50	0.0	0.0	2.50	2.50	2.50	2.50	2.50	100.00

22

CALM= 0.27 M/S

PERCENT DATA RECOVERY = 55.6

OVERALL STABILITY CLASS FREQUENCIES IN PERCENT

STABILITY:	A	B	C	D	E	F	G	ALL
FREQUENCY:	0.0	15.0	42.5	10.0	30.0	2.5	0.0	100.0

OVERALL WIND SPEED FREQUENCIES IN PERCENT

WIND SPEED (M/S):	CALM	CALM-.5	.5-.75	.75-1.0	1.0-1.5	1.5-2.0	2.0-3.0	3.0-5.0	5.0-10.0	>10.0	VARIABLE
FREQUENCY:	0.0	0.0	0.0	0.0	22.5	0.0	7.5	5.0	20.0	25.0	5.0
CUMULATIVE FREQ:	0.0	0.0	0.0	15.0	37.5	37.5	45.0	50.0	70.0	95.0	

PROGRAM: JFREQ   VERSION: 3   DATED: FEBRUARY 1982   RUN DATE: FRIDAY   MAY 7, 1982

SAMPLE RUN : INPUT FILE = DATA1 (SEE SAMPLE OUTPUT FOR PROGRAM PRINT)

LEVEL OF WIND DATA: 10.0 METERS   DELTA T LAYER: 60.0- 10.0 METERS

DISTRIBUTION OF VARIABLE WINDS

U (M/S)	A	B	C	D	E	F	G	TOTAL
CALM	0.0	0.0	0.0	0.0	0.0	0.0	0.0	0.0
CALM-.5	0.0	0.0	0.0	0.0	0.0	0.0	0.0	0.0
.5-.75	0.0	0.0	0.0	0.0	0.0	0.0	0.0	0.0
.75-1.0	0.0	0.0	0.0	0.0	0.0	0.0	0.0	0.0
1.0-1.5	0.0	0.0	0.0	0.0	0.0	0.0	0.0	0.0
1.5-2.0	0.0	0.0	0.0	0.0	0.0	0.0	0.0	0.0
2.0-3.0	0.0	0.0	0.0	0.0	0.0	0.0	0.0	0.0
3.0-5.0	0.0	0.0	0.0	0.0	0.00	0.0	0.00	0.00
5.0-10.0	0.0	0.0	0.0	0.0	5.00	0.0	0.00	5.00
>10.0	0.0	0.0	0.0	0.0	0.00	0.0	0.00	0.00
TOTAL	0.0	0.0	0.0	0.0	5.00	0.0	0.0	5.00

23

5.0 MISS

5.1 Description of Program

This program summarizes the periods of occurrence of missing hourly values of wind direction, wind speed, temperature, dew point, delta-T and precipitation for data in the NRC Standard Format.

5.2 Input Cards

Card	Column	Format	Variable	Description
1	1-72	18A4	TITLE	Title that will be printed at top of output.
2	1-6	3I2	JY, JM, JD	Starting year, month and day.
	7	1X		Blank.
	8-13	3I2	KY, KM, KD	Ending year, month and day.

5.3 Discussion of Output

The program MISS summarizes the lengths of the missing periods, the number of occurrences of missing data, the total number of hours of missing data, the longest period of missing data, the total number of hours checked and the percent data recovery.

5.4 Implementation

Input Units
    1 - data file of hourly metoerological data in the NRC Standard Format
    5 - input cards 1 and 2

Output Units
    - defaults to printer

5.5 Subroutine Flow Chart

```
MAIN ────── BLNK
      ├── CHK
      └── IDAT
```

5.6 Subroutine Descriptions

Except for MAIN, all subroutines are listed alphabetically.

MAIN

The main part of the program, reads in the data, makes all summaries and prints out the results.

BLNK

Checks for and converts blank data fields to 9999.9.

CHK

This routine categorizes the occurrence intervals of the missing data into periods of 1,2,3,4,5,6,7-11, 12-23, 24-47, 48-71, 72-95, 96-119 and greater then 119 hours.

IDAT

This routine converts a given month and day to an equivalent Julian day.

5.7 Sample Output

PROGRAM: MISS   VERSION: 2   DATED: FEBRUARY 1982   RUN DATE: FRIDAY   MAY 14, 1982

SITE:

          TEST   DATA

CONTAINS DATA FROM DECEMBER 1980 TO JANUARY 1891

HOURLY DATA CODED 0100 TO 2400

****

INPUT OPTIONS:

TITLE: SAMPLE RUN : INPUT FILE = DATA1   (SEE SAMPLE OUTPUT FOR PROGRAM PRINT)

STARTING DATE: 80 12 30
ENDING DATE: 81   1   7

27

PROGRAM: MISS   VERSION: 2   DATED: FEBRUARY 1982   RUN DATE: FRIDAY   MAY 14, 1982

SAMPLE RUN : INPUT FILE = DATA1 (SEE SAMPLE OUTPUT FOR PROGRAM PRINT)

HOURLY SUMMARY OF MISSING DATA

PERIOD OF OCCURRENCE (HOURS)	110.0 METERS				60.0 METERS				10.0 METERS				TEMPERATURE DIFFERENCE (DEGREES C/100METERS)			PRECIP. (mm)
	WIND DIR (DEG)	WIND SPEED (M/S)	TEMP (C)	DEW POINT (C)	WIND DIR (DEG)	WIND SPEED (M/S)	TEMP (C)	DEW POINT (C)	WIND DIR (DEG)	WIND SPEED (M/S)	TEMP (C)	DEW POINT (C)	110.0-10.0	110.0-60.0	60.0-10.0	
1	1	3	3	0	2	4	0	0	1	7	2	3	9	2	2	8
2	1	0	0	0	1	0	3	0	0	3	0	0	0	2	2	0
3	1	0	0	0	0	0	0	0	2	1	0	0	0	0	0	0
4	0	0	0	0	0	0	0	0	0	0	0	0	0	0	0	0
5	0	0	0	0	0	0	0	0	1	0	0	0	0	0	0	0
6	0	0	0	0	0	0	0	0	0	1	0	0	0	0	0	0
7-11	0	0	0	0	0	0	0	0	0	0	0	0	0	0	0	0
12-23	0	0	0	0	0	0	0	0	0	0	0	0	0	0	0	0
24-47	0	0	0	0	0	0	0	0	0	0	0	0	0	0	0	0
43-71	0	0	0	0	0	0	0	0	0	0	0	0	0	0	0	0
72-95	0	0	0	0	0	0	0	1	0	0	0	0	0	0	0	0
96-119	0	0	0	0	0	0	0	0	0	0	0	0	0	0	0	0
>120	0	0	0	0	0	0	0	0	0	0	0	0	0	0	0	1
LONGEST CASE	3	1	1	0	2	1	2	72	5	6	0	1	1	2	2	1
TOTAL HOURS MISSING	6	3	3	0	4	4	6	72	12	22	0	3	9	6	6	8
TOTAL HOURS	72	72	72	72	72	72	72	72	72	72	72	72	72	72	72	72
PERCENT DATA RECOVERY	91.7	95.8	95.8	100.0	94.4	94.4	91.7	0.0	83.3	69.4	100.0	95.8	87.5	91.7	91.7	88.9

28

6.0 PRECP

6.1 Description of Program

This program will summarize precipitation data by occurrence, intensity, stability class and month and day.

6.2 Input Cards

Card	Column	Format	Variable	Description
1	1-72	18A4	TITLE	Title to be printed on output.
2	1	I1	IS	Delta-T interval for stability determination. IS=1: upper-lower IS=2: upper-intermediate IS=3: intermediate-lower
	2	1x		Blank
	3-8	3I2	LY1, LM1, LD1	Starting year, month and day
	9	1x		Blank
	10-15	3I2	LY2, LM2, LD2	Ending year, month and day

6.3 Discussion of Output

Three tables are printed out which summarize precipitation amounts by month and day, precipitation occurrences by intensity and month, and precipitation occurrences by stability and intensity. Also given is the percent data recovery for precipitation.

6.4 Implementation

Input Units
    1 - data file of hourly meteorlogical data in the NRC Standard Format
    5 - input cards 1 and 2

Output Units
    - defaults to printer

6.5 Subroutine Flow Chart

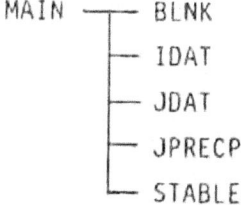

```
MAIN ─┬─ BLNK
      ├─ IDAT
      ├─ JDAT
      ├─ JPRECP
      └─ STABLE
```

6.6 Subroutine Descriptions

Except for MAIN, all subroutines are listed alphabetically.

MAIN

The main part of the program reads in the data, makes all summaries and prints out the results.

BLNK

Checks for and converts blank data fields to 9999.9.

IDAT

This routine converts a given month and day to an equivalenet Julian day.

JDAT

This routine converts a given Julian day to an equivalent month and day.

JPRECP

This routine categorizes hourly precipitation by intensity.

STABLE

This routine computes the stability class from atmospheric temperature gradient (delta-T) as follows.

Delta-T ($^\circ$C/100m)	Category	Stability Class
$\Delta T \leq -1.9$	1	A
$-1.9 < \Delta T \leq -1.7$	2	B
$-1.7 < \Delta T \leq -1.5$	3	C
$-1.5 < \Delta T \leq -0.5$	4	D
$-0.5 < \Delta T \leq 1.5$	5	E
$1.5 < \Delta T \leq 4.0$	6	F
$4.0 < \Delta T$	7	G

6.7 Sample Output

PROGRAM: PRECP   VERSION: 2   DATED: FEBRUARY 1982

SITE: TEST DATA

CONTAINS DATA FROM DECEMBER 1980 TO JANUARY 1891

HOURLY DATA CODED 0100 TO 2400

****

TITLE: SAMPLE RUN : INPUT FILE = DATA1 (SEE SAMPLE OUTPUT FOR PROGRAM PRINT)

START DATE: 80 12 30
END   DATE: 81 1 2

HOURS VALID PRECIPITATION: 64
TOTAL HOURS EXAMINED: 72
PERCENT DATA RECOVERY: 88.9

32

PROGRAM: PRECP   VERSION: 2   DATED: FEBRUARY 1982   RUN DATE: FRIDAY   MAY 21, 1982

SAMPLE RUN : INPUT FILE = DATA1   (SEE SAMPLE OUTPUT FOR PROGRAM PRINT)

PRECIPITATION SUMMARIZED BY MONTH AND DAY IN MILLIMETERS

DAY	JAN	FEB	MAR	APR	MAY	JUN	JUL	AUG	SEP	OCT	NOV	DEC
1	46.2	0.0	0.0	0.0	0.0	0.0	0.0	0.0	0.0	0.0	0.0	0.0
2	1.0	0.0	0.0	0.0	0.0	0.0	0.0	0.0	0.0	0.0	0.0	0.0
3	0.0	0.0	0.0	0.0	0.0	0.0	0.0	0.0	0.0	0.0	0.0	0.0
4	0.0	0.0	0.0	0.0	0.0	0.0	0.0	0.0	0.0	0.0	0.0	0.0
5	0.0	0.0	0.0	0.0	0.0	0.0	0.0	0.0	0.0	0.0	0.0	0.0
6	0.0	0.0	0.0	0.0	0.0	0.0	0.0	0.0	0.0	0.0	0.0	0.0
7	0.0	0.0	0.0	0.0	0.0	0.0	0.0	0.0	0.0	0.0	0.0	0.0
8	0.0	0.0	0.0	0.0	0.0	0.0	0.0	0.0	0.0	0.0	0.0	0.0
9	0.0	0.0	0.0	0.0	0.0	0.0	0.0	0.0	0.0	0.0	0.0	0.0
10	0.0	0.0	0.0	0.0	0.0	0.0	0.0	0.0	0.0	0.0	0.0	0.0
11	0.0	0.0	0.0	0.0	0.0	0.0	0.0	0.0	0.0	0.0	0.0	0.0
12	0.0	0.0	0.0	0.0	0.0	0.0	0.0	0.0	0.0	0.0	0.0	0.0
13	0.0	0.0	0.0	0.0	0.0	0.0	0.0	0.0	0.0	0.0	0.0	0.0
14	0.0	0.0	0.0	0.0	0.0	0.0	0.0	0.0	0.0	0.0	0.0	0.0
15	0.0	0.0	0.0	0.0	0.0	0.0	0.0	0.0	0.0	0.0	0.0	0.0
16	0.0	0.0	0.0	0.0	0.0	0.0	0.0	0.0	0.0	0.0	0.0	0.0
17	0.0	0.0	0.0	0.0	0.0	0.0	0.0	0.0	0.0	0.0	0.0	0.0
18	0.0	0.0	0.0	0.0	0.0	0.0	0.0	0.0	0.0	0.0	0.0	0.0
19	0.0	0.0	0.0	0.0	0.0	0.0	0.0	0.0	0.0	0.0	0.0	0.0
20	0.0	0.0	0.0	0.0	0.0	0.0	0.0	0.0	0.0	0.0	0.0	0.0
21	0.0	0.0	0.0	0.0	0.0	0.0	0.0	0.0	0.0	0.0	0.0	0.0
22	0.0	0.0	0.0	0.0	0.0	0.0	0.0	0.0	0.0	0.0	0.0	0.0
23	0.0	0.0	0.0	0.0	0.0	0.0	0.0	0.0	0.0	0.0	0.0	0.0
24	0.0	0.0	0.0	0.0	0.0	0.0	0.0	0.0	0.0	0.0	0.0	0.0
25	0.0	0.0	0.0	0.0	0.0	0.0	0.0	0.0	0.0	0.0	0.0	0.0
26	0.0	0.0	0.0	0.0	0.0	0.0	0.0	0.0	0.0	0.0	0.0	0.0
27	0.0	0.0	0.0	0.0	0.0	0.0	0.0	0.0	0.0	0.0	0.0	0.0
28	0.0	0.0	0.0	0.0	0.0	0.0	0.0	0.0	0.0	0.0	0.0	0.0
29	0.0		0.0	0.0	0.0	0.0	0.0	0.0	0.0	0.0	0.0	0.0
30	0.0		0.0	0.0	0.0	0.0	0.0	0.0	0.0	0.0	0.0	2.8
31	0.0		0.0		0.0		0.0	0.0		0.0		162.0
TOTAL	47.2	0.0	0.0	0.0	0.0	0.0	0.0	0.0	0.0	0.0	0.0	164.8

TOTAL=   212.0 MM

33

SAMPLE RUN : INPUT FILE = DATA1   (SEE SAMPLE OUTPUT FOR PROGRAM PRINT)

PRECIPITATION OCCURRENCES SUMMARIZED BY MONTH AND INTENSITY IN HOURS

INTENSITY (MM)	JAN	FEB	MAR	APR	MAY	JUN	JUL	AUG	SEP	OCT	NOV	DEC
0.0	24	0	0	0	0	0	0	0	0	0	0	25
>0.0- .25	0	0	0	0	0	0	0	0	0	0	0	3
>.25- .50	0	0	0	0	0	0	0	0	0	0	0	2
>.50- .75	1	0	0	0	0	0	0	0	0	0	0	1
>.75-1.00	1	0	0	0	0	0	0	0	0	0	0	1
>1.0-2.00	2	0	0	0	0	0	0	0	0	0	0	0
>2.0-3.00	0	0	0	0	0	0	0	0	0	0	0	0
>3.0-4.00	0	0	0	0	0	0	0	0	0	0	0	0
>4.0-5.00	0	0	0	0	0	0	0	0	0	0	0	0
>5.0-7.5	0	0	0	0	0	0	0	0	0	0	0	0
>7.5-10.	1	0	0	0	0	0	0	0	0	0	0	0
>10.-15.	0	0	0	0	0	0	0	0	0	0	0	0
>15.-20.	0	0	0	0	0	0	0	0	0	0	0	0
>20.-25.	1	0	0	0	0	0	0	0	0	0	0	1
>25.-30.	0	0	0	0	0	0	0	0	0	0	0	0
>30.-40.	1	0	0	0	0	0	0	0	0	0	0	0
>40.	0	0	0	0	0	0	0	0	0	0	0	2
TOTAL HRS	29	0	0	0	0	0	0	0	0	0	0	35
PERCENT	45.3	0.0	0.0	0.0	0.0	0.0	0.0	0.0	0.0	0.0	0.0	54.7

34

PROGRAM: PRECP   VERSION: 2   DATED: FEBRUARY 1982   RUN DATE: FRIDAY   MAY 21, 1982

SAMPLE RUN : INPUT FILE = DATA1 (SEE SAMPLE OUTPUT FOR PROGRAM PRINT)

DELTA-T INTERVAL: 60.0- 10.0 METERS

PRECIPITATION OCCURRENCES SUMMARIZED BY STABILITY AND INTENSITY IN HOURS

INTENSITY (MM)	STABILITY CLASS							MISS	TOTAL	PERCENT	CUMULATIVE PERCENT
	A	B	C	D	E	F	G				
0.0	4	6	17	10	3	2	2	5	49	76.56	76.6
>0.0-.25	0	0	0	0	3	0	0	0	3	4.69	81.3
>.25-.50	0	0	0	2	0	0	0	0	2	3.13	84.4
>.50-.75	0	0	0	1	0	0	0	0	1	1.56	85.9
>.75-1.0	1	0	0	1	0	0	0	0	2	3.13	89.1
>1.0-2.0	0	0	0	0	2	0	0	0	2	3.13	92.2
>2.0-3.0	0	0	0	0	0	0	0	0	0	0.00	92.2
>3.0-4.0	0	0	0	0	0	0	0	0	0	0.00	92.2
>4.0-5.0	0	0	0	0	0	0	0	0	0	0.00	92.2
>5.0-7.5	0	0	0	0	0	0	0	0	0	0.00	92.2
>7.5-10.	0	0	0	0	2	0	0	0	2	3.13	95.3
>10.-15.	0	0	0	0	0	0	0	0	0	0.00	95.3
>15.-20.	0	0	0	0	0	0	0	0	0	0.00	95.3
>20.-25.	0	0	0	0	0	0	0	0	0	0.00	95.3
>25.-30.	0	0	0	0	0	0	0	0	0	0.00	95.3
>30.-40.	0	0	0	0	1	0	0	0	1	1.56	96.9
>40.	0	0	0	0	2	0	0	0	2	3.13	100.0
HRS WITH PRECIP	1	0	0	4	10	0	0	0	15		
PERCENT	6.67	0.0	0.0	26.67	66.67	0.0	0.0	0.0		23.44	
TOTAL HRS	5	6	17	14	13	2	2	5	64		
PERCENT	7.8	9.4	26.6	21.9	20.3	3.1	3.1	7.8			

35

7.0 PRINT

7.1 Description of Program

This program produces a listing of the following parameters from a data file in the NRC Standard Format: wind direction, wind speed, sigma theta, temperature, dew point, delta-T and precipitation.

7.2 Input Cards

Card	Column	Format	Variable	Description
1	1-72	18A4	TITLE	Title to be printed on each page.
2	1-6	I6	IS	Start date for printing data in order of year, month an day (3I2).
	7	1X		Blank.
	8-13	I6	IE	End date for printing data in order of year, month and day (3I2).

7.3 Discussion of Output

The data is printed with a title and header on each page. There are 53 data records per page printed across 132 columns with each record preceeded by the year, month, day and hour. The stability class (A, B,..., G) is also given for sigma theta and delta-T data.

Missing data are printed out as follows:

	Missing data	Blank data field
wind speed	99.9	-99.9
wind direction	999	-99
sigma theta	999.9	-99.9
temperature	999.9	-99.9
dew point	999.9	-99.9
delta-T	99.9	-99.9
precipitation	999.9	-99.9

7.4 Implementation

Input Units
    1 - data file of hourly meteorological data in the NRC Standard Format
    5 - input cards 1 and 2.

Output Units
    - defaults to printer

7.5 Subroutine Flow Chart

```
MAIN ──┬── BLNK
       ├── JDAT
       ├── SIGMA
       └── STABLE
```

7.6 Subroutine Descriptions

Except for MAIN, all subroutines are listed alphabetically.

MAIN

The main part of the program reads in the data, calls all subroutines, and prints out the data.

BLNK

Checks for blank data fields and sets codes for missing data.

JDAT

This routine converts a given Julian day to an equivalent month and day.

SIGMA

This routine computes stability class from the horizontal deviation of wind direction (sigma theta) as follows.

Sigma theta (degrees)	Category	Stability Class
$22.5 \leq \sigma\theta$	1	A
$17.5 \leq \sigma\theta < 22.5$	2	B
$12.5 \leq \sigma\theta < 17.5$	3	C
$7.5 \leq \sigma\theta < 12.5$	4	D
$3.8 \leq \sigma\theta < 7.5$	5	E
$2.1 \leq \sigma\theta < 3.8$	6	F
$\sigma\theta < 2.1$	7	G

STABLE

This routine computes the stability class from atmospheric temperature gradient (delta-T) as follows.

Delta-T (°C/100m)	Category	Stability Class
$\Delta T \leq -1.9$	1	A
$-1.9 < \Delta T \leq -1.7$	2	B
$-1.7 < \Delta T \leq -1.5$	3	C
$-1.5 < \Delta T \leq -0.5$	4	D
$-0.5 < \Delta T \leq 1.5$	5	E
$1.5 < \Delta T \leq 4.0$	6	F
$4.0 < \Delta T$	7	G

7.7 Sample Output

PROGRAM: PRINT   DATED: MARCH 1982   VERSION: 2   RUN DATE: THURSDAY   MAY 13, 1982

SITE: TEST DATA

CONTAINS DATA FROM DECEMBER 1980 TO JANUARY 1891

HOURLY DATA CODED 0100 TO 2400

****

TITLE: SAMPLE RUN - INPUT FILE = DATA1

DATES SPECIFIED TO BE PRINTED:
   START DATE: 801230
   END DATE: 810102

PROGRAM: PRINT   DATED: MARCH 1982   VERSION: 2   RUN DATE: THURSDAY   MAY 13, 1982

SAMPLE RUN   -   INPUT FILE = DATA1

				110.0 METERS					60.0 METERS					10.0 METERS					TEMPERATURE DIFFERENCE (DEGREES C/100METERS)			
YR	MN	DY	HR	WD (DEG)	WS (M/S)	SIGMA (DEG)	TEMP (C)	DEWPT (C)	WD (DEG)	WS (M/S)	SIGMA (DEG)	TEMP (C)	DEWPT (C)	WD (DEG)	WS (M/S)	SIGMA (DEG)	TEMP (C)	DEWPT (C)	110.0-10.0	110.0-60.0	60.0-10.0	PRECIP (MM)
80	12	30	12	180	1.0	5.5 E	20.0	15.0	175	1.0	7.5 D	21.0	999.9	170	1.0	10.0 D	25.0	15.0	2.0 F	1.0 E	1.0 E	0.1
80	12	30	13	200	5.0	1.0 G	21.0	17.0	180	2.0	5.0 E	21.0	999.9	90	10.0	15.0 C	25.0	12.0	1.0 E	0.5 E	0.3 E	0.2
80	12	30	14	220	7.0	5.0 E	20.0	18.0	20	5.0	5.0 E	21.0	999.9	90	20.0	20.0 B	26.0	10.0	0.2 E	0.1 E	0.1 E	0.1
80	12	30	15	220	10.0	1.0 G	20.0	15.0	15	10.0	1.0 G	24.0	999.9	90	20.0	25.0 A	27.5	12.0	-2.0 A	-1.0 D	-1.0 D	0.4
80	12	30	16	220	12.0	0.5 G	20.0	19.0	10	10.0	2.0 G	25.0	999.9	90	20.0	30.0 A	28.0	10.0	-2.5 A	-1.2 D	-1.2 D	0.5
80	12	30	17	300	18.0	1.0 G	23.0	21.0	5	12.0	1.9 G	26.0	999.9	90	20.0	35.0 A	30.0	12.0	-2.6 A	-1.3 D	-1.4 D	0.6
80	12	30	18	320	15.0	1.5 G	20.0	18.0	1	5.0	2.1 F	26.5	999.9	90	20.0	9.0 D	25.0	15.0	-2.7 A	-1.3 D	-1.4 D	0.9
80	12	30	19	330	16.0	1.6 G	20.0	19.0	0	0.5	2.2 F	25.5	999.9	90	20.0	5.0 E	24.0	24.0	-2.8 A	-1.4 D	-1.5 C	0.0
80	12	30	20	340	10.0	1.7 G	20.0	19.9	36	0.1	2.3 F	25.0	999.9	90	20.0	4.0 E	23.0	23.0	-2.9 A	-1.4 D	-1.5 C	0.0
80	12	30	21	350	9.0	1.8 G	20.0	20.0	0	0.2	2.4 F	23.0	999.9	80	10.0	3.0 F	22.0	21.0	-3.0 A	-1.5 C	-1.5 C	0.0
80	12	30	22	351	9.1	1.9 G	21.0	20.0	360	0.3	2.5 F	22.5	999.9	70	5.0	2.0 G	21.0	21.0	-3.1 A	-1.5 C	-1.6 C	0.0
80	12	30	23	352	9.2	1.0 G	22.0	20.0	359	0.4	2.6 F	22.0	999.9	60	2.5	1.0 G	20.0	19.0	-3.2 A	-1.6 C	-1.6 C	0.0
80	12	30	24	353	9.3	0.9 G	22.0	10.0	358	0.5	2.7 F	20.0	999.9	50	1.3	0.5 G	22.0	19.0	-3.3 A	-1.6 C	-1.6 C	0.0
80	12	31	1	354	9.4	0.8 G	21.0	10.0	357	0.6	2.8 F	20.0	999.9	40	1.2	0.3 G	20.0	19.0	-3.4 A	-1.7 B	-1.7 B	0.0
80	12	31	2	355	9.5	0.7 G	21.0	11.0	356	0.7	2.9 F	19.0	999.9	30	1.1	0.2 G	15.0	12.0	-3.5 A	-1.8 B	-1.7 B	0.0
80	12	31	3	356	9.6	0.6 G	20.0	13.0	355	0.8	3.0 F	18.0	999.9	20	1.0	0.1 G	14.0	16.0	-3.6 A	-2.0 A	-1.6 C	0.0
80	12	31	4	357	9.7	0.5 G	999.9	12.0	354	0.9	0.1 G	17.0	999.9	20	99.9	0.0 G	14.0	15.0	-3.7 A	-2.1 A	-1.9 A	0.0
80	12	31	5	358	9.8	0.4 G	20.0	11.0	353	1.0	3.1 F	16.0	999.9	21	99.9	0.5 G	13.0	999.9	99.9 -	-2.0 A	-2.5 A	0.0
80	12	31	6	359	9.9	0.9 G	19.0	11.0	352	1.1	3.2 F	15.0	999.9	999	10.0	1.1 G	19.0	18.0	-2.2 A	-1.1 D	-1.2 D	999.9
80	12	31	7	360	10.0	1.0 G	12.0	11.0	350	1.2	3.3 F	14.0	999.9	999	5.0	1.5 G	20.0	19.0	-1.0 D	-1.0 D	-1.0 D	0.0
80	12	31	8	1	11.0	1.1 G	13.0	12.0	350	1.4	3.4 F	999.9	999.9	999	99.9	999.9 -	20.0	19.5	-1.0 D	-0.5 D	-0.5 D	0.0
80	12	31	9	1	11.0	1.1 G	12.0	11.0	340	13.0	3.5 F	999.9	999.9	10	10.0	1.4 G	21.0	20.0	-0.4 E	-0.2 E	-0.2 E	0.0
80	12	31	10	2	12.0	10.0 D	14.0	11.0	300	16.5	3.6 F	20.0	999.9	90	9.0	13.0 B	22.0	22.0	-0.1 E	-0.1 E	0.0 E	999.9
80	12	31	11	30	13.0	12.5 C	14.5	14.0	180	21.0	3.7 F	20.5	999.9	90	99.9	19.5 B	21.0	20.0	0.0 E	0.1 E	0.1 E	12.0
80	12	31	12	180	1.0	5.5 E	20.0	15.0	175	1.0	7.5 D	21.0	999.9	170	1.0	10.0 D	25.0	15.0	2.0 F	1.0 E	1.0 E	50.0
80	12	31	13	200	5.0	1.0 G	21.0	17.0	180	2.0	5.0 E	21.0	999.9	20	10.0	15.0 C	25.0	12.0	1.0 E	0.5 E	0.3 E	100.0
80	12	31	14	999	7.0	999.9 -	20.0	18.0	20	40.0	5.0 E	21.0	999.9	90	99.9	20.0 B	26.0	10.0	0.2 E	0.1 E	0.1 E	0.0
80	12	31	15	999	10.0	999.9 -	20.0	15.0	70	10.0	1.0 G	24.0	999.9	90	99.9	25.0 A	27.5	12.0	-2.0 A	-1.0 D	-1.0 D	0.0
80	12	31	16	220	12.0	999.9 -	20.0	19.0	100	10.0	2.0 G	25.0	999.9	90	99.9	30.0 A	28.0	10.0	-2.5 A	-1.2 D	-1.2 D	0.0
80	12	31	17	999	10.0	999.9 -	20.0	21.0	5	110.0	1.9 G	26.0	999.9	110	99.9	35.0 A	30.0	12.0	99.9 -	-1.3 D	-1.4 D	0.0
80	12	31	18	999	15.0	999.9 -	20.0	18.0	130	5.0	2.1 F	26.5	999.9	130	99.9	9.0 D	25.0	15.0	-2.7 A	99.9 -	-1.4 D	0.0
80	12	31	19	999	16.0	999.9 -	20.0	19.0	150	0.5	2.2 F	25.5	999.9	90	99.9	5.0 E	24.0	24.0	-2.8 A	-1.4 D	99.9 -	0.0
80	12	31	20	340	10.0	1.7 G	20.0	19.9	36	0.1	2.3 F	25.0	999.9	180	20.0	4.0 E	23.0	23.0	99.9 -	99.9 -	-1.5 C	0.0
80	12	31	21	350	9.0	1.8 G	20.0	20.0	0	0.2	2.4 F	23.0	999.9	200	10.0	3.0 F	22.0	21.0	-3.0 A	99.9 -	99.9 -	0.0
80	12	31	22	351	9.1	1.9 G	21.0	20.0	360	0.3	2.5 F	22.5	999.9	220	5.0	2.0 G	21.0	21.0	99.9 -	-1.5 C	99.9 -	0.0
80	12	31	23	352	9.2	1.0 G	22.0	20.0	359	0.4	2.6 F	22.0	999.9	250	2.5	1.0 G	20.0	19.0	-3.2 A	1.4 E	-1.6 C	0.0
80	12	31	24	353	9.3	0.9 G	22.0	10.0	358	0.5	2.7 F	20.0	999.9	260	1.3	0.5 G	20.0	19.0	-3.3 A	1.5 E	1.6 F	0.0
81	1	1	1	354	9.4	0.8 G	21.0	10.0	357	0.6	2.8 F	20.0	999.9	290	1.2	0.3 G	20.0	19.0	-3.4 A	-1.7 B	-1.7 B	0.0
81	1	1	2	355	9.5	0.7 G	21.0	11.0	999	99.9	999.9 -	19.0	999.9	310	1.1	0.2 G	15.0	12.0	-3.5 A	-1.8 B	-1.7 B	0.0
81	1	1	3	356	9.6	0.6 G	20.0	13.0	999	0.8	3.0 F	18.0	999.9	20	1.0	0.1 G	14.0	14.0	-3.6 A	-2.0 A	-1.6 C	0.0
81	1	1	4	357	9.7	0.5 G	999.9	12.0	354	99.9	0.1 G	17.0	999.9	20	99.9	0.0 G	14.0	15.0	5.0 G	4.1 G	3.9 F	0.0
81	1	1	5	358	9.8	0.4 G	20.0	11.0	353	1.0	3.1 F	16.0	999.9	21	99.9	0.5 G	13.0	999.9	99.9 -	4.8 G	7.5 G	0.0
81	1	1	6	359	99.9	0.9 G	19.0	11.0	352	99.9	3.2 F	15.0	999.9	999	99.9	1.1 G	19.0	18.0	-2.2 A	-1.1 D	-1.2 D	999.9
81	1	1	7	360	10.0	1.0 G	12.0	11.0	350	1.2	3.3 F	14.0	999.9	999	5.0	1.5 G	20.0	19.0	-1.0 D	-1.0 D	-1.0 D	0.0
81	1	1	8	999	11.0	1.1 G	13.0	12.0	999	1.4	3.4 F	999.9	999.9	999	99.9	999.9 -	20.0	19.5	-1.0 D	-0.5 D	-5.0 A	0.0
81	1	1	9	1	11.0	1.1 G	12.0	11.0	340	13.0	3.5 F	999.9	999.9	10	10.0	1.4 G	21.0	20.0	-0.4 E	-0.2 E	45.0 G	0.0
81	1	1	10	2	12.0	10.0 D	14.0	11.0	300	16.5	3.6 F	20.0	999.9	90	9.0	15.0 B	22.0	22.0	-0.1 E	-0.1 E	0.0 E	999.9
81	1	1	11	30	13.0	12.5 C	14.5	14.0	180	24.0	3.7 F	20.5	999.9	90	99.9	19.5 B	21.0	20.0	0.0 E	0.1 E	0.1 E	1.2
81	1	1	12	180	1.0	5.5 E	20.0	15.0	175	1.0	7.5 D	21.0	999.9	150	1.0	10.0 D	25.0	15.0	2.0 F	1.0 E	1.0 E	2.0
81	1	1	13	200	5.0	1.0 G	21.0	17.0	180	2.0	5.0 E	21.0	999.9	90	10.0	15.0 C	25.0	12.0	1.0 E	0.5 E	0.3 E	11.0
81	1	1	14	220	7.0	5.0 E	20.0	18.0	999	5.0	5.0 E	21.0	999.9	90	99.9	20.0 D	26.0	10.0	99.9 -	0.1 E	0.1 E	32.0
81	1	1	15	220	99.9	1.0 G	20.0	15.0	15	10.0	1.0 G	24.0	999.9	90	99.9	25.0 A	27.5	12.0	-2.0 A	99.9 -	-1.0 D	0.0

PROGRAM: PRINT   DATED: MARCH 1982   VERSION: 2   RUN DATE: THURSDAY   MAY 13, 1982

SAMPLE RUN - INPUT FILE = DATA1

YR	MN	DY	HR	110.0 METERS					60.0 METERS					10.0 METERS					TEMPERATURE DIFFERENCE (DEGREES C/100METERS)			PRECIP
				WD (DEG)	WS (M/S)	SIGMA (DEG)	TEMP (C)	DEWPT (C)	WD (DEG)	WS (M/S)	SIGMA (DEG)	TEMP (C)	DEWPT (C)	WD (DEG)	WS (M/S)	SIGMA (DEG)	TEMP (C)	DEWPT (C)	110.0- 60.0	110.0- 10.0	60.0- 10.0	(MM)
81	1	1	16	220	12.0	0.5 G	20.0	19.0	10	10.0	2.0 G	25.0	999.9	-90	20.0	30.0 A	26.0	10.0	-2.5 A	-1.2 D	-1.2 D	0.0
81	1	1	17	300	18.0	1.0 G	20.0	21.0	5	12.0	1.9 G	26.0	999.9	20	20.0	35.0 A	30.0	12.0	99.9 -	99.9 -	99.9 -	0.0
81	1	1	18	320	15.0	-99.9 I	20.0	13.0	1	5.0	2.1 F	26.5	999.9	90	20.0	-9.0 I	25.0	15.0	-2.7 A	99.9 -	99.9 -	-99.9
81	1	1	19	330	16.0	1.6 G	20.0	19.0	0	0.5	2.2 F	25.5	999.9	90	20.0	0.0 G	24.0	24.0	-2.8 A	-1.4 D	-1.5 C	0.0
81	1	1	20	340	10.0	1.7 G	20.0	19.0	36	0.1	2.3 F	25.0	999.9	80	10.0	4.0 E	23.0	23.0	-2.9 A	-1.5 D	-1.5 C	0.0
81	1	1	21	351	-99.9 I	1.8 G	23.0	20.0	360	0.3	2.4 F	23.0	999.9	70	5.0	3.0 G	21.0	21.0	-3.0 A	-1.5 C	-1.5 C	0.0
81	1	1	22	352	9.2	1.9 G	21.0	20.0	359	0.3	2.5 F	22.0	999.9	60	1.3	1.0 G	20.0	19.0	-99.9 I	-1.6 C	-1.6 C	0.0
81	1	1	23	353	9.3	0.8 G	22.0	20.0	353	0.5	2.6 F	22.0	999.9	50	1.2	0.5 G	20.0	19.0	-3.2 A	-1.6 C	-1.6 B	0.0
81	1	1	24	354	9.4	0.7 G	22.0	10.0	357	0.7	2.8 F	20.0	999.9	40	1.0	0.3 G	15.0	12.0	-3.3 A	-1.7 B	-1.7 B	0.0
81	1	2	1	355	9.5	0.6 G	21.0	11.0	356	0.8	3.0 F	20.0	999.9	30	1.0	0.1 G	14.0	14.0	-3.5 A	-1.7 A	-1.7 C	0.0
81	1	2	2	356	9.6	0.5 G	20.0	13.0	354	0.9	3.1 F	18.0	999.9	328	1.0	0.2 G	14.0	15.0	-3.6 A	-1.3 A	-1.6 C	-99.9
81	1	2	3	357	9.7	0.4 G	999.9	12.0	353	1.0	3.2 F	17.0	999.9	23	99.9	0.1 G	13.0	999.0	-3.7 A	-2.0 A	-1.9 A	0.0
81	1	2	4	358	9.8	0.0 G	20.0	11.0	352	1.2	3.3 F	16.0	999.9	21	99.9	0.5 G	19.0	18.0	99.9 A	-2.1 A	-2.5 A	999.9
81	1	2	5	360	10.0	1.0 G	19.0	11.0	350	1.4	3.4 F	16.0	999.9	999	10.0	1.5 G	20.0	19.5	-2.2 A	-2.0 D	-1.2 D	0.0
81	1	2	6	1	11.0	1.1 G	12.0	12.0	350	13.0	3.5 F	14.0	999.9	999	5.0	999.9 I	20.0	19.5	-1.0 D	-1.0 A	-1.0 G	0.0
81	1	2	7	2	12.0	10.0 D	13.0	11.0	340	16.0	3.6 F	999.9	999.9	8888	99.9	1.4 G	21.0	20.0	99.9 D	-2.0 A	5.0 G	999.9
81	1	2	8	30	13.0	12.5 C	14.5	14.0	180	21.0	3.7 F	20.5	999.9	8880	9.0	18.0 D	22.0	22.0	-0.4 E	-0.2 E	-0.2 E	0.0
81	1	2	9											30	99.9	19.5 B	21.0	20.0	-0.1 E	-0.1 E	-0.0 E	999.9
81	1	2	10																0.0 E	0.1 E	-2.0 A	1.0

41

PROGRAM: PRINT   DATED: MARCH 1982   VERSION: 2   RUN DATE: THURSDAY   MAY 13, 1982

SITE: TEST DATA

CONTAINS DATA FROM DECEMBER 1980 TO JANUARY 1981

BAD DATA DATES INSERTED TO CHECK PROGRAM DATE

HOURLY DATA CODED 0100 TO 2400

TITLE: SAMPLE RUN   -   INPUT FILE = DATA2

DATES SPECIFIED TO BE PRINTED:
    START DATE: 0
    END DATE: 999999

42

PROGRAM: PRINT   DATED: MARCH 1982   VERSION: 2   RUN DATE: THURSDAY   MAY 13, 1932

SAMPLE RUN   -   INPUT FILE = DATA2

YR	MN	DY	HR	110.0 METERS WD (DEG)	WS (M/S)	SIGMA (DEG)	TEMP (C)	DEWPT (C)	60.0 METERS WD (DEG)	WS (M/S)	SIGMA (DEG)	TEMP (C)	DEWPT (C)	10.0 METERS WD (DEG)	WS (M/S)	SIGMA (DEG)	TEMP (C)	DEWPT (C)	TEMPERATURE DIFFERENCE (DEGREES C/10 METERS) 110.0- 10.0	110.0- 60.0	60.0- 10.0	PRECIP (MM)

YR	MN	DY	HR	110.0 METERS				60.0 METERS				10.0 METERS				TEMPERATURE DIFFERENCE (DEGREES C/100METERS)			PRECIP
				WD (DEG)	WS (M/S)	SIGMA (DEG)	TEMP (C)	DEWPT (C)	WD (DEG)	WS (M/S)	SIGMA (DEG)	TEMP (C)	DEWPT (C)	WD (DEG)	WS (M/S)	SIGMA (DEG)	TEMP (C)	DEWPT (C)	110.0-60.0	110.0-10.0	60.0-10.0	(MM)

8.0 QA

8.1 Description of Program

This is a quality assurance program for checking hourly meteorological data in the NRC Standard Format. Meteorological variables that can be checked are; wind speed, wind direction, temperature, dew point, temperature gradient and precipitation. Data are read and checked one hour at a time with the date, time and a description of the problem printed out if any questionable occurrences are found.

8.2 Input Cards

Card	Column	Format	Variable	Descriptions
1	1	I1	LEV	Specifies the level(s) of data to be checked. LEV=1: upper LEV=2: upper and lower LEV=3: upper, intermediate and lower LEV=4: lower
	2	I1	IS	Specifies which delta-T intervals are to be checked. IS=0: NONE IS=1: U-L IS=2: U-I IS=3: I-L IS=4: U-L and U-I IS=5: U-L and I-L IS=6: U-I and I-L IS=7: U-L, U-I and I-L where U=upper I=intermediate and L=lower
	3	I1	IW	Check wind speed and direction IW=1: check IW=0: do not check
	4	I1	IT	Check temperature IT=1: check IT=0: do not check
	5	I1	ID	Check dew point ID=1: check ID=0: do not check IF ID=1, IT must equal 1

Card	Column	Format	Variable	Description
1	6	I1	IP	Check precipitation IP=1: check IP=0: do not check
	7	1X		Blank
	8-13	3I2	LY1, LM1, LD1	Year, month and day checking is to begin
	14	1X		Blank
	15-20	3I2	LY2, LM2, LD2	Year, month and day checking is to end
2	1-72	18A4	TITLE(18)	Title to be printed on each page of the output

8.3 Discussion of Output

Whenever the program flags a potential error in the data, a description of the problem along with the data and time of occurrence is printed out. For errors that have persisted for an extended period of time, the last hour of that time period will be the time printed. The occurrence of valid data will cause any checking of an error over an extended time period to end. At the end of the printed output, the summaries from checking the wind speed and direction data will be printed. Also printed will be the maximum and minimum values for all levels of wind speed and direction, temeprature, dew point, delta-T and precipitation, and the number of hours they were based on. When all checking of data and printing has been completed, a statement indicating successful completion will be printed.

8.4 Implementation

Input Units
    1 - data file of hourly meteorological data
    5 - input cards 1 and 2

Output Units
    - defaults to printer

8.5 <u>Subroutine Flow Chart</u>

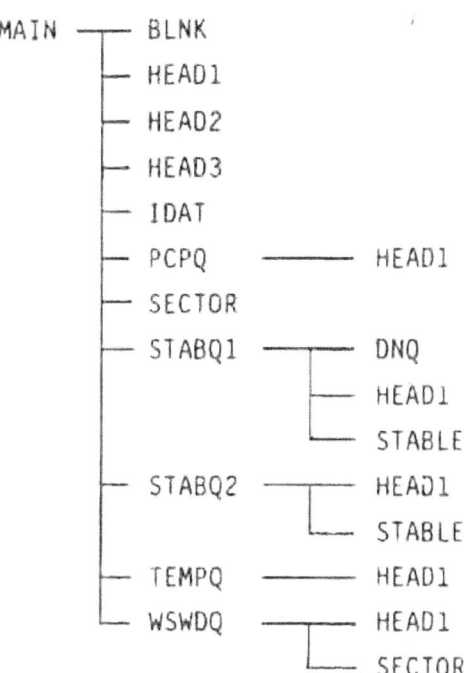

```
MAIN ──── BLNK
      ├── HEAD1
      ├── HEAD2
      ├── HEAD3
      ├── IDAT
      ├── PCPQ ──────── HEAD1
      ├── SECTOR
      ├── STABQ1 ──┬── DNQ
      │            ├── HEAD1
      │            └── STABLE
      ├── STABQ2 ──┬── HEAD1
      │            └── STABLE
      ├── TEMPQ ──────── HEAD1
      └── WSWDQ ──┬── HEAD1
                  └── SECTOR
```

8.6 <u>Subroutine Descriptions</u>

Except for MAIN, all subroutines are listed alphabetically.

MAIN

The main program initializes all data, reads the input cards, prints out the input information, reads and writes the title from the data file, reads the data from the data file and calls the appropriate subroutines for checking the data.

BLNK

Checks for and converts blank data fields to 9999.9.

DNQ

This routine checks for F or G stability during the day and A, B, or C stability at night for IS=1.   Day is defined as:

    December 24 - March   22 (Winter); hours 8-17
    March   23 - June   21 (Spring); hours 7-18
    June   22 - September 20 (Summer); hours 6-19
    September 21 - December   23 (Fall);   hours 7-18

All other hours are defined as night.

HEAD1

This routine prints a header, page number and title at the top of each page of the output.

47

HEAD2

This routine prints out the input parameters that were specified.

HEAD3

This routine prints out the summarizations of the wind speed and wind direction data compiled in subroutine WSWDQ. HEAD3 is called only after the last data record has been checked.

IDAT

This routine converts a specified month and day to an equivalent Julian day.

PCPQ

This routine checks precipitation data as follows for IP=1.

- Checks for precipitation occurring greater than 8 consecutive hours.

- Checks for 1 hour of precipitation greater than or equal to 25mm (1 inch).

SECTOR

This routine distributes the wind direction data into 16 sectors centered on the principle compass points using the following equation.

SECTOR = 1+[(DIR+11.25)/22.5]

if SECTOR = 17, change to SECTOR = 1

where SECTOR = direction sector wind is blowing from
              (SECTOR should be truncated to nearest whole number)
      DIR = direction wind is blowing from (degrees)

Variable wind directions are treated as missing data.

STABLE

This routine computes the stability class from atmospheric temperature gradient (delta-T) as follows.

Delta-T ($^\circ$C/100m)	Category	Stability Class
$\Delta T \leq -1.9$	1	A
$-1.9 < \Delta T \leq -1.7$	2	B
$-1.7 < \Delta T \leq -1.5$	3	C
$-1.5 < \Delta T \leq -0.5$	4	D
$-0.5 < \Delta T \leq 1.5$	5	E
$1.5 < \Delta T \leq 4.0$	6	F
$4.0 < \Delta T$	7	G

STABQ1

This routine makes the following three checks on the stability measurements for IS=1.

- Checks for the wind speed at any of the levels specified to be greater than 7.5 m/sec during unstable (A,B,C) or stable (F,G) conditions.

- Checks for delta-T less than -3.4°C/100 meters (autoconvective lapse rate).

- Checks for unstable (A,B,C) or stable (F,G) conditions during precipitation.

STABQ2

This routine makes the following stability checks for IS=1.

- Checks for a greater than 3 stability class jump for two consecutive hours.

- Checks for the same stability class for 12 or more consecutive hours.

- Checks for a greater than 2 stability class difference between two temperature gradient intervals for the same hour.

TEMPQ

This routine checks both temperature and dew point at all specified levels for IT=1. The checks that are made are as follows.

- The same temperature for 8 or more consecutive hours.

- Dew point greater than temperature if ID=1.

- Temperature minus dew point greater than 5°C during precipitation if ID=1.

- Temperature equal to dew point for 8 or more consecutive hours if ID=1.

WSWDQ

This subroutine makes the following checks on wind direction and wind speed for IW=1.

For each level:

- Checks for wind speed greater than 25 m/sec.

- Checks for wind direction from the same sector for more than 8 consecutive hours.

49

If more then one level is to checked:

- Totals up the cases where the wind direction is the same at any two levels.

- Totals up the cases where the wind speed is the same at any two levels.

- Totals up the cases where the wind speed is greater than 2.5, 5.0 and 7.5 m/sec at either of two levels while the wind direction between the two levels is greater than 22.5 degrees.

- Checks for the wind speed at the lower of any two levels to be greater than the wind speed at the upper of any two levels.

8.7 Sample Output

SAMPLE RUN : INPUT FILE = DATA1 (SEE SAMPLE OUTPUT FOR PROGRAM PRINT)

CHECK FOLLOWING LEVEL(S) OF DATA:
    LOWER
    INTERMEDIATE
    UPPER

CHECK FOLLOWING DELTA-T INTERVALS:
    INTERMEDIATE MINUS   LOWER
    UPPER   MINUS   INTERMEDIATE
    UPPER   MINUS   LOWER

CHECK WIND SPEED AND DIRECTION: YES

CHECK TEMPERATURE: YES

CHECK DEW POINT: YES

CHECK PRECIPITATION: YES

CHECK DATA: BEGINING -   80 12 30
          ENDING   -   81   1   2

SITE:
    TEST DATA

52

CONTAINS DATA FROM DECEMBER 1980 TO JANUARY 1891

HOURLY DATA CODED 0100 TO 2400

****

SAMPLE RUN : INPUT FILE = DATA1   (SEE SAMPLE OUTPUT FOR PROGRAM PRINT)

```
YR DAY HOUR
80 365 1200  HEIGHT= 10.0M  TEMPERATURE GREATER THEN DEW POINT BY 10.0 DEGREES C DURING PRECIPITATION OF    0.1 MM
80 365 1200  PRECIPITATION OCCURED DURING STABILITY CLASS F BETWEEN 110.0M AND 10.0M
80 365 1300  STABILITY CLASS   F DURING DAY BETWEEN 110.0M AND 10.0M
80 365 1300  HEIGHT= 10.0M  TEMPERATURE GREATER THEN DEW POINT BY 13.0 DEGREES C DURING PRECIPITATION OF    0.2 MM
80 365 1400  HEIGHT= 10.0M  TEMPERATURE GREATER THEN DEW POINT BY 16.0 DEGREES C DURING PRECIPITATION OF    0.1 MM
80 365 1500  HEIGHT= 10.0M  TEMPERATURE GREATER THEN DEW POINT BY 15.5 DEGREES C DURING PRECIPITATION OF    0.4 MM
80 365 1500  WIND SPEED GREATER THEN 7.5M/SEC FOR STABILITY CLASS A BETWEEN 110.0M AND 10.0M
80 365 1500  PRECIPITATION OCCURED DURING STABILITY CLASS A OVER ONE HOUR PERIOD
80 365 1500  STABILITY CLASS JUMPED FROM E TO A BETWEEN 110.0M AND 10.0M
80 365 1500  STABILITY FOR 110.0M MINUS 10.0M IS   A WHILE STABILITY FOR 60.0M MINUS 10.0M IS D
80 365 1500  STABILITY FOR 110.0M MINUS 10.0M IS   A WHILE STABILITY FOR 110.0M MINUS 60.0M IS D
80 365 1600  HEIGHT= 10.0M  TEMPERATURE GREATER THEN DEW POINT BY 18.0 DEGREES C DURING PRECIPITATION OF    0.5 MM
80 365 1600  WIND SPEED GREATER THEN 7.5M/SEC FOR STABILITY CLASS A BETWEEN 110.0M AND 10.0M
80 365 1600  PRECIPITATION OCCURED DURING STABILITY CLASS A BETWEEN 110.0M AND 10.0M
80 365 1600  STABILITY FOR 110.0M MINUS 10.0M IS   A WHILE STABILITY FOR 60.0M MINUS 10.0M IS D
80 365 1600  STABILITY FOR 110.0M MINUS 10.0M IS   A WHILE STABILITY FOR 110.0M MINUS 60.0M IS D
80 365 1700  HEIGHT= 10.0M  TEMPERATURE GREATER THEN DEW POINT BY 18.0 DEGREES C DURING PRECIPITATION OF    0.6 MM
80 365 1700  HEIGHT= 110.0M  DEW POINT ( 21.0 ) IS GREATER THEN TEMPERATURE ( 20.0 )
80 365 1700  WIND SPEED GREATER THEN 7.5M/SEC FOR STABILITY CLASS A BETWEEN 110.0M AND 10.0M
80 365 1700  STABILITY FOR 110.0M MINUS 10.0M IS   A WHILE STABILITY FOR 60.0M MINUS 10.0M IS D
80 365 1700  STABILITY FOR 110.0M MINUS 10.0M IS   A WHILE STABILITY FOR 110.0M MINUS 60.0M IS D
80 365 1800  HEIGHT= 10.0M  TEMPERATURE GREATER THEN DEW POINT BY 10.0 DEGREES C DURING PRECIPITATION OF    3.9 MM
80 365 1800  PRECIPITATION OCCURED DURING STABILITY CLASS A BETWEEN 110.0M AND 10.0M
80 365 1800  STABILITY CLASS A DURING NIGHT BETWEEN 110.0M AND 10.0M
80 365 1800  WIND SPEED GREATER THEN 7.5M/SEC FOR STABILITY CLASS A BETWEEN 110.0M AND 10.0M
80 365 1900  WIND SPEED GREATER THEN 7.5M/SEC FOR STABILITY CLASS C DURING NIGHT BETWEEN 110.0M AND 10.0M
80 365 1900  STABILITY CLASS A DURING NIGHT BETWEEN 110.0M AND 10.0M
80 365 1900  STABILITY FOR 110.0M MINUS 10.0M IS   A WHILE STABILITY FOR 60.0M MINUS 10.0M IS D
80 365 1900  WIND SPEED GREATER THEN 7.5M/SEC FOR STABILITY CLASS A BETWEEN 110.0M AND 10.0M
80 365 2000  STABILITY CLASS C DURING NIGHT BETWEEN 60.0M AND 10.0M
80 365 2000  WIND SPEED GREATER THEN 7.5M/SEC FOR STABILITY CLASS C DURING NIGHT BETWEEN 110.0M AND 10.0M   D
80 365 2000  STABILITY FOR 110.0M MINUS 10.0M IS   A WHILE STABILITY FOR 110.0M MINUS 60.0M IS D
80 365 2000  WIND SPEED GREATER THEN 7.5M/SEC FOR STABILITY CLASS A BETWEEN 110.0M AND 10.0M
80 365 2100  STABILITY CLASS C DURING NIGHT BETWEEN 110.0M AND 10.0M
80 365 2100  WIND SPEED GREATER THEN 7.5M/SEC FOR STABILITY CLASS C DURING NIGHT BETWEEN 110.0M AND 10.0M
80 365 2100  STABILITY CLASS C DURING NIGHT BETWEEN 110.0M AND 60.0M
80 365 2100  WIND SPEED GREATER THEN 7.5M/SEC FOR STABILITY CLASS C DURING NIGHT BETWEEN 110.0M AND 60.0M
80 365 2100  STABILITY CLASS C DURING NIGHT BETWEEN 60.0M AND 10.0M
80 365 2100  WIND FROM SECTOR E FOR PREVIOUS 9 HOUR PERIOD
80 365 2200  HEIGHT= 10.0M  TEMPERATURE= 20.0DEGREES C FOR STABILITY CLASS
80 365 2200  WIND SPEED GREATER THEN 7.5M/SEC FOR STABILITY CLASS A BETWEEN 110.0M AND 10.0M
80 365 2200  STABILITY CLASS C DURING NIGHT BETWEEN 110.0M AND 60.0M
80 365 2200  WIND SPEED GREATER THEN 7.5M/SEC FOR STABILITY CLASS C DURING NIGHT BETWEEN 110.0M AND 60.0M
80 365 2300  STABILITY CLASS A DURING NIGHT BETWEEN 110.0M AND 10.0M
80 365 2300  WIND SPEED GREATER THEN 7.5M/SEC FOR STABILITY CLASS C DURING NIGHT BETWEEN 110.0M AND 60.0M
```

SAMPLE RUN : INPUT FILE = DATA1   (SEE SAMPLE OUTPUT FOR PROGRAM PRINT)

YR	DAY	HOUR	
80	365	2300	STABILITY CLASS C DURING NIGHT BETWEEN 110.0M AND 60.0M
80	365	2300	STABILITY CLASS C DURING NIGHT BETWEEN 60.0M AND 10.0M
80	365	2400	WIND SPEED GREATER THEN 7.5M/SEC FOR STABILITY CLASS A BETWEEN 110.0M AND 10.0M
80	365	2400	WINDSPEED GREATER THEN 7.5M/SEC FOR STABILITY CLASS C BETWEEN 110.0M AND 60.0M
80	365	2400	STABILITY CLASS C DURING NIGHT BETWEEN 60.0M AND 10.0M
80	365	2400	WIND SPEED GREATER THEN 7.5M/SEC FOR STABILITY CLASS A BETWEEN 110.0M AND 10.0M
80	366	100	STABILITY CLASS A DURING NIGHT BETWEEN 110.0M AND 10.0M
80	366	100	WIND SPEED GREATER THEN 7.5M/SEC FOR STABILITY CLASS B BETWEEN 110.0M AND 60.0M
80	366	100	STABILITY CLASS B DURING NIGHT BETWEEN 110.0M AND 60.0M
80	366	100	STABILITY CLASS B DURING NIGHT BETWEEN 60.0M AND 10.0M
80	366	200	WIND SPEED GREATER THEN 7.5M/SEC FOR STABILITY CLASS A BETWEEN 110.0M AND 10.0M
80	366	200	LAPSE RATE OF -3.5 DEGREES C/100METERS EXCEEDS THE AUTOCONVECTIVE LAPSE RATE
80	366	200	WIND SPEED GREATER THEN 7.5M/SEC FOR STABILITY CLASS B BETWEEN 110.0M AND 60.0M
80	366	200	STABILITY CLASS B DURING NIGHT BETWEEN 60.0M AND 10.0M
80	366	300	WIND SPEED GREATER THEN 7.5M/SEC FOR STABILITY CLASS A BETWEEN 110.0M AND 10.0M
80	366	300	LAPSE RATE OF -3.6 DEGREES C/100METERS EXCEEDS THE AUTOCONVECTIVE LAPSE RATE
80	366	300	WIND SPEED GREATER THEN 7.5M/SEC FOR STABILITY CLASS A BETWEEN 110.0M AND 60.0M
80	366	300	STABILITY CLASS A DURING NIGHT BETWEEN 110.0M AND 10.0M
80	366	300	STABILITY CLASS C DURING NIGHT BETWEEN 60.0M AND 10.0M
80	366	400	HEIGHT= 10.0M DEW POINT (15.0) IS GREATER THEN TEMPERATURE (14.0)
80	366	400	WIND SPEED GREATER THEN 7.5M/SEC FOR STABILITY CLASS A BETWEEN 110.0M AND 10.0M
80	366	400	LAPSE RATE OF -3.7 DEGREES C/100METERS EXCEEDS THE AUTOCONVECTIVE LAPSE RATE
80	366	400	WIND SPEED GREATER THEN 7.5M/SEC FOR STABILITY CLASS A BETWEEN 110.0M AND 60.0M
80	366	400	STABILITY CLASS A DURING NIGHT BETWEEN 110.0M AND 10.0M
80	366	500	WIND SPEED GREATER THEN 7.5M/SEC FOR STABILITY CLASS A BETWEEN 110.0M AND 60.0M
80	366	500	STABILITY CLASS A DURING NIGHT BETWEEN 110.0M AND 60.0M
80	366	500	STABILITY CLASS A DURING NIGHT BETWEEN 60.0M AND 10.0M
80	366	600	WIND SPEED GREATER THEN 7.5M/SEC FOR STABILITY CLASS A BETWEEN 110.0M AND 10.0M
80	366	600	STABILITY CLASS A DURING NIGHT BETWEEN 110.0M AND 10.0M
80	366	600	STABILITY FOR 110.0M MINUS 10.0M IS A WHILE STABILITY FOR 60.0M MINUS 10.0M IS D
80	366	800	STABILITY FOR 110.0M MINUS 60.0M IS A WHILE STABILITY FOR 110.0M MINUS 60.0M IS D
80	366	1000	HEIGHT= 60.0M WIND FROM SECTOR N FOR PREVIOUS 12 HOUR PERIOD
80	366	1000	HEIGHT= 110.0M WIND FROM SECTOR N FOR PREVIOUS 14 HOUR PERIOD
80	366	1200	HEIGHT= 10.0M TEMPERATURE GREATER THEN DEW POINT BY 10.0 DEGREES C DURING PRECIPITATION OF 50.0 MM
80	366	1200	PRECIPITATION OF 50.0M FELL IN THE GIVEN 1 HOUR PERIOD
80	366	1200	PRECIPITATION OCCURED DURING STABILITY CLASS F BETWEEN 110.0M AND 10.0M
80	366	1300	STABILITY CLASS F DURING DAY BETWEEN 110.0M AND 10.0M
80	366	1300	HEIGHT= 10.0M TEMPERATURE GREATER THEN DEW POINT BY 13.0 DEGREES C DURING PRECIPITATION OF 100.0 MM
80	366	1400	PRECIPITATION OF 100.0M FELL IN THE GIVEN 1 HOUR PERIOD
80	366	1500	HEIGHT= 60.0M WIND SPEED OF 40.0M/SEC OCCURRED
80	366	1500	WIND SPEED GREATER THEN 7.5M/SEC FOR STABILITY CLASS A BETWEEN 110.0M AND 10.0M
80	366	1500	STABILITY CLASS JUMPED FROM E TO A OVER ONE HOUR PERIOD BETWEEN 110.0M AND 10.0M
80	366	1500	STABILITY FOR 110.0M MINUS 10.0M IS A WHILE STABILITY FOR 60.0M MINUS 10.0M IS D
80	366	1600	STABILITY FOR 110.0M MINUS 10.0M IS A WHILE STABILITY FOR 110.0M MINUS 60.0M IS D
80	366	1600	WINDSPEED GREATER THEN 7.5M/SEC FOR STABILITY CLASS A BETWEEN 110.0M AND 10.0M
80	366	1600	STABILITY FOR 110.0M MINUS 10.0M IS A WHILE STABILITY FOR 60.0M MINUS 10.0M IS D
80	366	1600	STABILITY FOR 110.0M MINUS 10.0M IS A WHILE STABILITY FOR 110.0M MINUS 60.0M IS D

54

SAMPLE RUN : INPUT FILE = DATA1   (SEE SAMPLE OUTPUT FOR PROGRAM PRINT)

YR	DAY	HOUR		
80	366	1700	HEIGHT= 110.0M DEW POINT (21.0) IS GREATER THEN TEMPERATURE (20.0)	D
80	366	1700	STABILITY FOR 110.0M MINUS 10.0M IS A WHILE STABILITY FOR 60.0M MINUS 10.0M IS	D
80	366	1700	STABILITY FOR 110.0M MINUS 10.0M IS A WHILE STABILITY FOR 110.0M MINUS 60.0M IS	D
80	365	1800	WIND SPEED GREATER THEN 7.5M/SEC FOR STABILITY CLASS A BETWEEN 110.0M AND 10.0M	
80	365	1800	STABILITY CLASS A DURING NIGHT BETWEEN 110.0M AND 10.0M	D
80	366	1800	STABILITY FOR 110.0M MINUS 10.0M IS A WHILE STABILITY FOR 60.0M MINUS 10.0M IS	D
80	366	1800	STABILITY FOR 110.0M MINUS 10.0M IS A WHILE STABILITY FOR 110.0M MINUS 60.0M IS	D
80	366	1900	WIND SPEED GREATER THEN 7.5M/SEC FOR STABILITY CLASS A BETWEEN 110.0M AND 10.0M	
80	366	1900	STABILITY CLASS A DURING NIGHT BETWEEN 110.0M AND 10.0M	D
80	366	1900	STABILITY FOR 110.0M MINUS 10.0M IS A WHILE STABILITY FOR 60.0M MINUS 10.0M IS	D
80	366	1900	STABILITY FOR 110.0M MINUS 10.0M IS A WHILE STABILITY FOR 110.0M MINUS 60.0M IS	D
80	366	2000	WIND SPEED GREATER THEN 7.5M/SEC FOR STABILITY CLASS C BETWEEN 60.0M AND 10.0M	
80	366	2000	STABILITY CLASS C DURING NIGHT BETWEEN 60.0M AND 10.0M	D
80	366	2000	STABILITY FOR 110.0M MINUS 10.0M IS A WHILE STABILITY FOR 60.0M MINUS 10.0M IS	D
80	366	2000	STABILITY FOR 110.0M MINUS 10.0M IS A WHILE STABILITY FOR 110.0M MINUS 60.0M IS	D
80	366	2100	WIND SPEED GREATER THEN 7.5M/SEC FOR STABILITY CLASS A BETWEEN 110.0M AND 10.0M	
80	366	2100	HEIGHT= 10.0M TEMPERATURE= 20.0DEGREES C FOR PREVIOUS & HOUR PERIOD	
80	366	2100	STABILITY CLASS C DURING NIGHT BETWEEN 110.0M AND 60.0M	D
80	366	2200	WIND SPEED GREATER THEN 7.5M/SEC FOR STABILITY CLASS C BETWEEN 110.0M AND 60.0M	
80	366	2200	STABILITY FOR 110.0M MINUS 10.0M IS A WHILE STABILITY FOR 60.0M MINUS 10.0M IS	D
80	366	2200	STABILITY FOR 110.0M MINUS 10.0M IS A WHILE STABILITY FOR 110.0M MINUS 60.0M IS	D
80	366	2300	WIND SPEED GREATER THEN 7.5M/SEC FOR STABILITY CLASS A BETWEEN 110.0M AND 10.0M	
80	366	2300	STABILITY CLASS A DURING NIGHT BETWEEN 110.0M AND 10.0M	D
80	366	2300	STABILITY CLASS C DURING NIGHT BETWEEN 60.0M AND 10.0M	E
80	366	2400	WIND SPEED GREATER THEN 7.5M/SEC FOR STABILITY CLASS A BETWEEN 110.0M AND 10.0M	
80	366	2400	STABILITY FOR 110.0M MINUS 10.0M IS A WHILE STABILITY FOR 60.0M MINUS 10.0M IS	E
80	366	2400	STABILITY FOR 110.0M MINUS 10.0M IS A WHILE STABILITY FOR 110.0M MINUS 60.0M IS	E
81	1	100	WIND SPEED GREATER THEN 7.5M/SEC FOR STABILITY CLASS A BETWEEN 110.0M AND 10.0M	
81	1	100	WIND SPEED GREATER THEN 7.5M/SEC FOR STABILITY CLASS B BETWEEN 110.0M AND 60.0M	
81	1	100	STABILITY CLASS B DURING NIGHT BETWEEN 110.0M AND 60.0M	
81	1	100	STABILITY CLASS JUMPED FROM F TO B OVER ONE HOUR PERIOD BETWEEN 60.0M AND 10.0M	
81	1	200	WIND SPEED GREATER THEN 7.5M/SEC FOR STABILITY CLASS A BETWEEN 110.0M AND 10.0M	
81	1	200	LAPSE RATE OF -3.5 DEGREES C/100METERS EXCEEDS THE AUTOCONVECTIVE LAPSE RATE	
81	1	200	STABILITY CLASS A DURING NIGHT BETWEEN 110.0M AND 10.0M	
81	1	200	WIND SPEED GREATER THEN 7.5M/SEC FOR STABILITY CLASS B BETWEEN 110.0M AND 60.0M	
81	1	200	STABILITY CLASS B DURING NIGHT BETWEEN 110.0M AND 60.0M	
81	1	300	WIND SPEED GREATER THEN 7.5M/SEC FOR STABILITY CLASS A BETWEEN 60.0M AND 10.0M	
81	1	300	LAPSE RATE OF -3.6 DEGREES C/100METERS EXCEEDS THE AUTOCONVECTIVE LAPSE RATE	
81	1	300	STABILITY CLASS A DURING NIGHT BETWEEN 110.0M AND 10.0M	
81	1	300	STABILITY CLASS A DURING NIGHT BETWEEN 110.0M AND 60.0M	
81	1	300	STABILITY CLASS G DURING NIGHT BETWEEN 110.0M AND 10.0M	
81	1	400	HEIGHT= 10.0M DEW POINT (15.0) IS GREATER THEN TEMPERATURE (14.0)	
81	1	400	WIND SPEED GREATER THEN 7.5M/SEC FOR STABILITY CLASS G BETWEEN 110.0M AND 10.0M	
81	1	400	WIND SPEED GREATER THEN 7.5M/SEC FOR STABILITY CLASS G BETWEEN 60.0M AND 10.0M	

SAMPLE RUN : INPUT FILE = DATA1   (SEE SAMPLE OUTPUT FOR PROGRAM PRINT)

YR	DAY	HOUR	
81	1	400	STABILITY CLASS JUMPED FROM A TO G OVER ONE HOUR PERIOD BETWEEN 110.0M AND 10.0M
81	1	400	STABILITY CLASS JUMPED FROM A TO G OVER ONE HOUR PERIOD BETWEEN 110.0M AND 60.0M
81	1	500	WIND SPEED GREATER THEN 7.5M/SEC FOR STABILITY CLASS G BETWEEN 110.0M AND 60.0M
81	1	600	STABILITY CLASS A DURING NIGHT BETWEEN 110.0M AND 10.0M
81	1	600	STABILITY FOR 110.0M MINUS 10.0M IS G WHILE STABILITY FOR 60.0M MINUS 10.0M IS D
81	1	600	STABILITY FOR 110.0M MINUS 10.0M IS G WHILE STABILITY FOR 110.0M MINUS 60.0M IS D
81	1	700	HEIGHT= 110.0M WIND FROM SECTOR H FOR PREVIOUS 11 HOUR PERIOD
81	1	700	LAPSE RATE OF -5.0 DEGREES C/100METERS EXCEEDS THE AUTOCONVECTIVE LAPSE RATE
81	1	800	STABILITY FOR 110.0M MINUS 10.0M IS D WHILE STABILITY FOR 60.0M MINUS 10.0M IS A
81	1	800	STABILITY FOR 110.0M MINUS 60.0M IS D WHILE STABILITY FOR 110.0M MINUS 60.0M IS A
81	1	900	STABILITY FOR 110.0M MINUS 60.0M IS E WHILE STABILITY FOR 60.0M MINUS 10.0M IS A
81	1	900	STABILITY FOR 110.0M MINUS 60.0M IS E WHILE STABILITY FOR 60.0M MINUS 10.0M IS A
81	1	1000	STABILITY FOR 110.0M MINUS 10.0M IS E WHILE STABILITY FOR 60.0M MINUS 10.0M IS A
81	1	1000	STABILITY FOR 110.0M MINUS 60.0M IS E WHILE STABILITY FOR 60.0M MINUS 10.0M IS A
81	1	1200	HEIGHT= 10.0M TEMPERATURE GREATER THEN DEW POINT BY 10.0 DEGREES C DURING PRECIPITATION OF 2.0 MM
81	1	1200	PRECIPITATION OCCURED DURING STABILITY CLASS F BETWEEN 110.0M AND 10.0M
81	1	1200	STABILITY CLASS F DURING DAY BETWEEN 110.0M AND 10.0M
81	1	1300	HEIGHT= 10.0M TEMPERATURE GREATER THEN DEW POINT BY 13.0 DEGREES C DURING PRECIPITATION OF 11.0 MM
81	1	1400	HEIGHT= 10.0M TEMPERATURE GREATER THEN DEW POINT BY 16.0 DEGREES C DURING PRECIPITATION OF 32.0 MM
81	1	1400	PRECIPITATION OF 32.0M FELL IN THE GIVEN 1 HOUR PERIOD
81	1	1600	WIND SPEED GREATER THEN 7.5M/SEC FOR STABILITY CLASS A BETWEEN 110.0M AND 10.0M
81	1	1600	STABILITY FOR 110.0M MINUS 10.0M IS A WHILE STABILITY FOR 110.0M MINUS 60.0M IS E
81	1	1700	HEIGHT= 110.0M DEW POINT (21.0) IS GREATER THEN TEMPERATURE (20.0)
81	1	1700	STABILITY FOR 110.0M MINUS 10.0M IS A WHILE STABILITY FOR 110.0M MINUS 60.0M IS D
81	1	1800	WIND SPEED GREATER THEN 7.5M/SEC FOR STABILITY CLASS A DURING NIGHT BETWEEN 110.0M AND 10.0M
81	1	1800	STABILITY FOR 110.0M MINUS 10.0M IS A WHILE STABILITY FOR 110.0M MINUS 60.0M IS D
81	1	1850	STABILITY FOR 110.0M MINUS 10.0M IS A WHILE STABILITY FOR 110.0M MINUS 60.0M IS E
81	1	1900	WIND SPEED GREATER THEN 7.5M/SEC FOR STABILITY CLASS A DURING NIGHT BETWEEN 110.0M AND 10.0M
81	1	1900	WIND SPEED GREATER THEN 7.5M/SEC FOR STABILITY CLASS A BETWEEN 50.0M AND 10.0M
81	1	1900	STABILITY CLASS C DURING NIGHT BETWEEN 110.0M AND 10.0M
81	1	2000	STABILITY FOR 110.0M MINUS 10.0M IS A WHILE STABILITY FOR 60.0M MINUS 10.0M IS C
81	1	2000	WIND SPEED GREATER THEN 7.5M/SEC FOR STABILITY CLASS A DURING NIGHT BETWEEN 110.0M AND 10.0M
81	1	2100	WIND SPEED GREATER THEN 7.5M/SEC FOR STABILITY CLASS A WHILE STABILITY FOR 110.0M MINUS 60.0M IS C
81	1	2100	STABILITY FOR 110.0M MINUS 10.0M IS A WHILE STABILITY FOR 60.0M MINUS 10.0M IS C
81	1	2100	WIND SPEED GREATER THEN 7.5M/SEC FOR STABILITY CLASS C DURING NIGHT BETWEEN 110.0M AND 10.0M
81	1	2100	STABILITY CLASS C DURING NIGHT BETWEEN 110.0M AND 60.0M
81	1	2100	HEIGHT= 110.0M TEMPERATURE= 20.0DEGREES C FOR PREVIOUS 8 HOUR PERIOD
81	1	2200	STABILITY CLASS C DURING NIGHT BETWEEN 110.0M AND 60.0M
81	1	2200	STABILITY CLASS C DURING NIGHT BETWEEN 50.0M AND 10.0M
81	1	2300	WIND SPEED GREATER THEN 7.5M/SEC FOR STABILITY CLASS A BETWEEN 110.0M AND 10.0M
81	1	2300	STABILITY CLASS C DURING NIGHT BETWEEN 110.0M AND 60.0M
81	1	2300	WIND SPEED GREATER THEN 7.5M/SEC FOR STABILITY CLASS C DURING NIGHT BETWEEN 110.0M AND 60.0M

SAMPLE RUN : INPUT FILE = DATA1   (SEE SAMPLE OUTPUT FOR PROGRAM PRINT)

YR	DAY	HOUR	
81	1	2300	STABILITY CLASS C DURING NIGHT BETWEEN 60.0M AND 10.0M
81	1	2400	WIND SPEED GREATER THEN 7.5M/SEC FOR STABILITY CLASS A BETWEEN 110.0M AND 10.0M
81	1	2400	STABILITY CLASS A DURING NIGHT BETWEEN 110.0M AND 10.0M
81	1	2400	WIND SPEED GREATER THEN 7.5M/SEC FOR STABILITY CLASS C BETWEEN 110.0M AND 50.0M
81	1	2400	STABILITY CLASS C DURING NIGHT BETWEEN 60.0M AND 10.0M
81	2	100	WIND SPEED GREATER THEN 7.5M/SEC FOR STABILITY CLASS A BETWEEN 110.0M AND 10.0M
81	2	100	STABILITY CLASS A DURING NIGHT BETWEEN 110.0M AND 10.0M
81	2	100	WIND SPEED GREATER THEN 7.5M/SEC FOR STABILITY CLASS B BETWEEN 110.0M AND 60.0M
81	2	100	STABILITY CLASS B DURING NIGHT BETWEEN 110.0M AND 60.0M
81	2	100	STABILITY CLASS B DURING NIGHT BETWEEN 60.0M AND 10.0M
81	2	200	WIND SPEED GREATER THEN 7.5M/SEC FOR STABILITY CLASS A
81	2	200	LAPSE RATE OF -3.5 DEGREES C/100METERS EXCEEDS THE AUTOCONVECTIVE LAPSE RATE BETWEEN 110.0M AND 10.0M
81	2	200	WIND SPEED GREATER THEN 7.5M/SEC FOR STABILITY CLASS B BETWEEN 110.0M AND 60.0M
81	2	200	STABILITY CLASS B DURING NIGHT BETWEEN 110.0M AND 60.0M
81	2	200	STABILITY CLASS B DURING NIGHT BETWEEN 60.0M AND 10.0M
81	2	300	WIND SPEED GREATER THEN 7.5M/SEC FOR STABILITY CLASS A
81	2	300	LAPSE RATE OF -3.6 DEGREES C/100METERS EXCEEDS THE AUTOCONVECTIVE LAPSE RATE BETWEEN 110.0M AND 10.0M
81	2	300	WIND SPEED GREATER THEN 7.5M/SEC FOR STABILITY CLASS A BETWEEN 110.0M AND 60.0M
81	2	300	STABILITY CLASS A DURING NIGHT BETWEEN 110.0M AND 60.0M
81	2	303	STABILITY CLASS A DURING NIGHT BETWEEN 60.0M AND 10.0M
81	2	400	STABILITY CLASS C DURING NIGHT BETWEEN 110.0M AND 60.0M
81	2	400	DEW POINT (10.0M) 15.0 IS GREATER THEN TEMPERATURE (14.0)
81	2	400	WIND SPEED GREATER THEN 7.5M/SEC FOR STABILITY CLASS A
81	2	400	LAPSE RATE OF -3.7 DEGREES C/100METERS EXCEEDS THE AUTOCONVECTIVE LAPSE RATE BETWEEN 110.0M AND 10.0M
81	2	400	WIND SPEED GREATER THEN 7.5M/SEC FOR STABILITY CLASS A BETWEEN 110.0M AND 60.0M
81	2	400	STABILITY CLASS A DURING NIGHT BETWEEN 110.0M AND 60.0M
81	2	500	STABILITY CLASS A DURING NIGHT BETWEEN 60.0M AND 10.0M
81	2	500	WIND SPEED GREATER THEN 7.5M/SEC FOR STABILITY CLASS A
81	2	500	STABILITY CLASS A DURING NIGHT BETWEEN 110.0M AND 60.0M
81	2	500	WIND SPEED GREATER THEN 7.5M/SEC FOR STABILITY CLASS A BETWEEN 110.0M AND 10.0M
81	2	600	STABILITY CLASS A DURING NIGHT BETWEEN 110.0M AND 10.0M
81	2	600	STABILITY FOR 110.0M MINUS 10.0M IS A WHILE STABILITY FOR 30.0M MINUS 10.0M IS D
81	2	600	STABILITY FOR 110.0M MINUS 10.0M IS A WHILE STABILITY FOR 110.0M MINUS 60.0M IS D
81	2	800	WIND SPEED GREATER THEN 7.5M/SEC FOR STABILITY CLASS A BETWEEN 110.0M AND 10.0M
81	2	800	STABILITY CLASS G DURING DAY BETWEEN 60.0M AND 10.0M
81	2	800	STABILITY FOR 110.0M MINUS 10.0M IS D WHILE STABILITY FOR 60.0M MINUS 10.0M IS G
81	2	800	STABILITY FOR 110.0M MINUS 60.0M IS D WHILE STABILITY FOR 60.0M MINUS 10.0M IS G A
81	2	900	HEIGHT= 60.0M WIND FROM SECTOR N FOR PREVIOUS 12 HOUR PERIOD BETWEEN 110.0M AND 60.0M
81	2	1000	STABILITY CLASS JUMPED FROM A TO N FOR PREVIOUS 14 HOUR PERIOD
81	2	1100	HEIGHT= 110.0M WIND FROM SECTOR A
81	2	1100	WIND SPEED GREATER THEN 7.5M/SEC FOR STABILITY CLASS A BETWEEN 60.0M AND 10.0M
81	2	1100	PRECIPITATION OCCURED DURING STABILITY CLASS E TO A OVER ONE HOUR PERIOD BETWEEN 60.0M AND 10.0M
81	2	1100	STABILITY CLASS JUMPED FROM E TO A BETWEEN 60.0M AND 10.0M
81	2	1100	STABILITY FOR 110.0M MINUS 10.0M IS E WHILE STABILITY FOR 60.0M MINUS 10.0M IS A
81	2	1100	STABILITY FOR 110.0M MINUS 60.0M IS E WHILE STABILITY FOR 60.0M MINUS 10.0M IS A

57

SAMPLE RUN : INPUT FILE = DATA1   (SEE SAMPLE OUTPUT FOR PROGRAM PRINT)

NUMBER OF OCCURRANCES OF WS AT 110.0M LOWER THEN THE WS AT 60.0M EQUALS   10

NUMBER OF OCCURRANCES OF WS AT 60.0M LOWER THEN THE WS AT 10.0M EQUALS   40

NUMBER OF OCCURRANCES OF WS AT 110.0M LOWER THEN THE WS AT 10.0M EQUALS   20

NUMBER OF OCCURRANCES OF WD AT 110.0M EQUAL TO WD AT 60.0M EQUALS   0

NUMBER OF OCCURRANCES OF WD AT 60.0M EQUAL TO WD AT 10.0M EQUALS   1

NUMBER OF OCCURRANCES OF WD AT 110.0M EQUAL TO WD AT 10.0M EQUALS   0

NUMBER OF OCCURRANCES OF WS AT 110.0M EQUAL TO WS AT 60.0M EQUALS   5

NUMBER OF OCCURRANCES OF WS AT 60.0M EQUAL TO WS AT 10.0M EQUALS   3

NUMBER OF OCCURRANCES OF WS AT 110.0M EQUAL TO WS AT 10.0M EQUALS   3

WD DIFFERENCE BETWEEN 110.0M AND 60.0M IS GREATER THEN OR EQUAL TO 22.5 DEGREES AND
  WS AT EITHER LEVEL IS GREATER THEN OR EQUAL TO 2.5M/SEC   OCCURRANCES= 29
  WS AT EITHER LEVEL IS GREATER THEN OR EQUAL TO 5.0M/SEC   OCCURRANCES= 29
  WS AT EITHER LEVEL IS GREATER THEN OR EQUAL TO 7.5M/SEC   OCCURRANCES= 28

WD DIFFERENCE BETWEEN 60.0M AND 10.0M IS GREATER THEN OR EQUAL TO 22.5 DEGREES AND
  WS AT EITHER LEVEL IS GREATER THEN OR EQUAL TO 2.5M/SEC   OCCURRANCES= 33
  WS AT EITHER LEVEL IS GREATER THEN OR EQUAL TO 5.0M/SEC   OCCURRANCES= 30
  WS AT EITHER LEVEL IS GREATER THEN OR EQUAL TO 7.5M/SEC   OCCURRANCES= 27

WD DIFFERENCE BETWEEN 110.0M AND 10.0M IS GREATER THEN OR EQUAL TO 22.5 DEGREES AND
  WS AT EITHER LEVEL IS GREATER THEN OR EQUAL TO 2.5M/SEC   OCCURRANCES= 49
  WS AT EITHER LEVEL IS GREATER THEN OR EQUAL TO 5.0M/SEC   OCCURRANCES= 49
  WS AT EITHER LEVEL IS GREATER THEN OR EQUAL TO 7.5M/SEC   OCCURRANCES= 47

SAMPLE RUN : INPUT FILE = DATA1   (SEE SAMPLE OUTPUT FOR PROGRAM PRINT)

SUMMARY OF MAXIMUM AND MINIMUM VALUES

	110.0 M			60.0 M			10.0 M		
	HRS	MIN	MAX	HRS	MIN	MAX	HRS	MIN	MAX
WIND DIRECTION (DEG)	66	1.0	360.0	63	5.0	360.0	60	10.0	328.0
WIND SPEED (M/S)	69	1.0	15.0	68	0.1	40.0	50	1.0	20.0
TEMPERATURE (DEG C)	69	12.0	22.0	66	14.0	26.5	72	13.0	30.0
MOISTURE (DEG C OR %)	72	10.0	21.0	0	999.9	-99.9	69	10.0	24.0

	110.0 - 10.0 M			110.0 - 60.0 M			60.0 - 10.0 M		
DELTA T (DEG C/100M)	63	-3.7	5.0	66	-2.1	4.8	66	-5.0	7.5

	GROUND LEVEL		
PRECIPITATION (MM)	64	0.0	100.0

9.0 STABQ

9.1 Description of Program

STABQ reads hourly values of temperature gradient (delta-T) or sigma theta from a data set in the NRC Standard Format and summarizes the data according to stability class and continuous periods of occurrence.

5.2 Input Cards

Card	Column	Format	Variable	Description
1	1-72	10A4	TITLE	Title that will be printed at top of each page of output.
2	1	I1	IS	Stability criteria: IS=1, Delta-T IS=2, Sigma Theta
	2-8	1x,3I2	JY, JM, JD	Starting year, month and day
	9-15	1x, 3I2	KY, KM, KD	Ending year, month and day

9.3 Discussion of Output

Three tables are printed; one for each of the possible stability levels available from the three measurement levels. Stability data is summarized by periods of occurrence with the longest single period of occurrence also given. If a missing data value is encoutnered, the period of occurrence will end.

9.4 Implementation

Input Units
      1 - data file of hourly meteorological data in the NRC Standard Format
      5 - input cards 1 and 2

Output Unit
      - defaults to printer

9.5 Subroutine Flow Chart

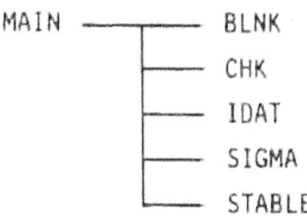

```
MAIN ──────┬───── BLNK
           ├───── CHK
           ├───── IDAT
           ├───── SIGMA
           └───── STABLE
```

9.6 Subroutine Descriptions

Except for MAIN all subroutines are listed alphabetically.

MAIN

The main part of the program reads in the data, makes all summaries and prints out the results.

BLNK

Checks for and converts blank data fields to 9999.9.

CHK

This routine categorizes the occurrence intervals of the stabilities into periods of 1,2,3,4,5,6,7-11, 12-23, 24-47, 48-71, 72-95, 96-119 and greater than 119 hours.

IDAT

This routine converts a specified month and day to an equivalent Julian day.

SIGMA

This routine computes stability class from the horizontal deviation of wind direction (sigma theta) as follows.

Sigma theta (degrees)	Category	Stability Class
$22.5 \leq \sigma\theta$	1	A
$17.5 \leq \sigma\theta < 22.5$	2	B
$12.5 \leq \sigma\theta < 17.5$	3	C
$7.5 \leq \sigma\theta < 12.5$	4	D
$3.8 \leq \sigma\theta < 7.5$	5	E
$2.1 \leq \sigma\theta < 3.8$	6	F
$\sigma\theta < 2.1$	7	G

STABLE

This routine computes the stability class from atmospheric temperature gradient (delta-T) as follows.

Delta-T (°C/100m)	Category	Stability Class
$\Delta T \leq -1.9$	1	A
$-1.9 < \Delta T \leq -1.7$	2	B
$-1.7 < \Delta T \leq -1.5$	3	C
$-1.5 < \Delta T \leq -0.5$	4	D
$-0.5 < \Delta T \leq 1.5$	5	E
$1.5 < \Delta T \leq 4.0$	6	F
$4.0 < \Delta T$	7	G

61

9.7 Sample Output

PROGRAM: STABQ   VERSION: 2   DATED: FEBRUARY 1982   RUN DATE: FRIDAY   MAY 7, 1982

TEST DATA
---- ----

CONTAINS DATA FROM DECEMBER 1980 TO JANUARY 1891

HOURLY DATA CODED 0100 TO 2400

****

INPUT OPTIONS:

TITLE. SAMPLE RUN : INPUT FILE = DATA1   (SEE SAMPLE OUTPUT FOR PROGRAM PRINT)

COMPUTE STABILITY BASED ON: DELTA-T

START DATE: 80 12 30
END   DATE: 81 1 2

63

PROGRAM: STABQ   VERSION: 2   DATED: FEBRUARY 1982   RUN DATE: FRIDAY   MAY 7, 1982

SAMPLE RUN : INPUT FILE = DATA1 (SEE SAMPLE OUTPUT FOR PROGRAM PRINT)

STABILITY BASED ON DELTA-T BETWEEN 110.0- 10.0 METERS

NUMBER OF OCCURENCES

PERIOD OF OCCURENCE (HOURS)	STABILITY						
	A	B	C	D	E	F	G
1	4	0	0	0	1	3	1
2	3	0	0	3	2	0	0
3	0	0	0	0	3	0	0
4	1	0	0	0	0	0	0
5	1	0	0	0	0	0	0
6	1	0	0	0	0	0	0
7-11	0	0	0	0	0	0	0
12-23	1	0	0	0	0	0	0
24-47	0	0	0	0	0	0	0
48-71	0	0	0	0	0	0	0
72-95	0	0	0	0	0	0	0
96-119	0	0	0	0	0	0	0
>120	0	0	0	0	0	0	0
LONGEST CASE	14	0	0	2	3	1	1

64

PROGRAM: STABQ   VERSION: 2   DATED: FEBRUARY 1982   RUN DATE: FRIDAY   MAY 7, 1982

SAMPLE RUN : INPUT FILE = DATA1   (SEE SAMPLE OUTPUT FOR PROGRAM PRINT)

STABILITY BASED ON DELTA-T BETWEEN 110.0- 60.0 METERS

NUMBER OF OCCURRENCES

PERIOD OF OCCURRENCE (HOURS)	STABILITY						
	A	B	C	D	E	F	G
1	2	0	1	2	0	0	0
2	0	3	0	2	1	0	1
3	2	0	0	3	2	0	0
4	0	0	2	0	0	0	0
5	0	0	0	0	0	0	0
6	0	0	0	1	2	0	0
7-11	0	0	0	0	0	0	0
12-23	0	0	0	0	0	0	0
24-47	0	0	0	0	0	0	0
48-71	0	0	0	0	0	0	0
72-95	0	0	0	0	0	0	0
96-115	0	0	0	3	0	0	0
>120	0	0	0	0	0	0	0
LONGEST CASE	3	2	6	6	6	0	2

65

PROGRAM: STABQ   VERSION: 2   DATED: FEBRUARY 1982   RUN DATE: FRIDAY   MAY 7, 1982

SAMPLE RUN : INPUT FILE = DATA1   (SEE SAMPLE OUTPUT FOR PROGRAM PRINT)

STABILITY BASED ON DELTA-T BETWEEN 60.0- 10.0 METERS

NUMBER OF OCCURENCES

PERIOD OF OCCURENCE (HOURS)	STABILITY						
	A	B	C	D	E	F	G
1	2	0	5	0	0	2	2
2	2	3	0	3	1	0	0
3	0	0	0	1	1	0	0
4	0	0	0	2	0	0	0
5	0	0	0	0	1	0	0
6	0	0	2	0	1	0	0
7-11	0	0	0	0	0	0	0
12-23	0	0	0	0	0	0	0
24-47	0	0	0	0	0	0	0
48-71	0	0	0	0	0	0	0
72-95	0	0	0	0	0	0	0
96-119	0	0	0	0	0	0	0
>120	0	0	0	0	0	0	0
LONGEST CASE	2	2	6	4	6	1	1

66

10.0 TDP

10.1 Description of Program

This program determines the average, minimum and maximum values of temperature, dew point, wind speed and wet bulb from hourly data in the NRC Standard Format. The average value for wind speed is the root-mean-square wind speed and wet bulb is calculated from temperature, dew point and barometric pressure.

10.2 Input Cards

Card	Column	Format	Variable	Description
1	1-72	18A4	TITLE	Title to be printed at the top of each page of the output.
2	1-10	F10.0	PBAR	Barometric pressure (inches of Mercury)
3	1-6	3I2	LY1, LM1, LD1	Start date (year, month and day)
	7	1x		Blank
	8-13	3I2	LY2, LM2, LD2	End date (year, month and day)

10.3 Discussion of Output

Printed output from TDP contains both monthly and annual summaries for all three possible levels in the NRC Standard Format. If a level has no available data, then the output will indicate all missing data. Also printed out are the number of valid data values that were used to determine each of the results.

Wet bulb temperature is calculated from temperature, dew point and the barometric pressure inputted on Card 2. If dew point is greater than temperature for a given hour, the dew point value is assumed to be invalid and not used.

Dew point is read from the field labeled "moisture" in the NRC Standard Format. In the event that dew point is not located there, the format of the read statement will have to be modified so that dew point will be read. Similarly if wet bulb were already available, the program would have to be modified not calculate it, but use it directly.

10.4 Implementation

Input Units
    1 - data file of hourly meterological data in the NRC Standard Format
    5 - input cards 1, 2, and 3

Output Units
    - defaults to printer

10.5 Subroutine Flow Chart

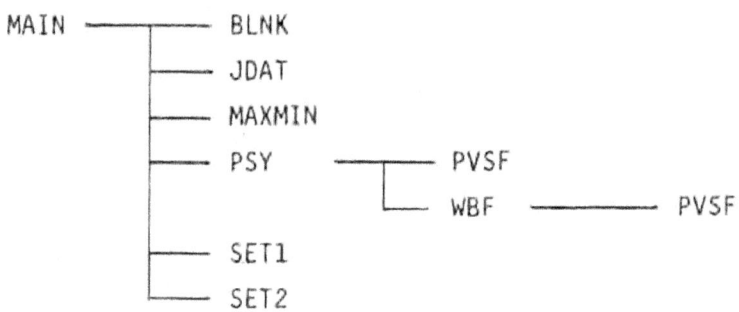

10.6 Subroutine Descriptions

Except for MAIN all subroutines are listed alphabetically.

MAIN

The main part of the program reads in all data, makes all summarizations and prints out the results.

BLNK

Checks for blank data fields and converts them to 9999.9.

JDAT

This routine converts a given Julian day to an equivalent month and day.

MAXMIN

This routine determines the maximum and minimum values on a monthly basis for each of the variables.

PSY

This routine calculates the wet bulb temperature (degrees F), humidity ratio (lb of water vapor/lb of dry air), enthalpy (BTU's/lb of dry air), volume (cubic feet/lb of dry air), vapor pressure (inches of Mercury) and relative humidity (fraction, not percent) from temperature (degrees F), dew point (Degrees F), and barometric pressure (inches of Mercury).

The source of this subroutine is: NUREG-0693, Analysis of Ultimate Heat Sink Cooling Ponds, by R. Codell and W. K. Nuttle, USNRC, November 1980, p. 104.

PVSF

This function calculates the vapor pressure of water (inches of Mercury) as a function of temperature (degrees F). The source of this function is: NUREG-0693, Analysis of Ultimate Heat Sink Cooling Ponds, by R. Codell and W. K. Nuttle, USNRC, November 1980, pp. 104-105.

SET1, SET2

These routines are used to initialize data.

WBF

This function approximates the wet bulb temperature (degrees F) from enthalpy (BTU's/lb of dry air) and barometric pressure (inches of Mercury). The source of this routine is: NUREG-0693, Analysis of Ultimate Heat Sink Cooling Ponds, by R. Codell and W. K. Nuttle, USNRC, November 1980, p. 105.

10.7 Sample Output

PROGRAM: TDP   VERSION: 3   DATED: MARCH 1982   RUN DATE: FRIDAY   MAY 7, 1982

SITE:

       TEST DATA

CONTAINS DATA FROM DECEMBER 1980 TO JANUARY 1891

HOURLY DATA CODED 0100 TO 2400

****

TITLE: SAMPLE RUN : INPUT FILE = DATA1 (SEE SAMPLE OUTPUT FOR PROGRAM PRINT)

INPUT DATA:

BAROMETRIC PRESSURE: 29.0

START DATE: 80 12 30
END   DATE: 81 1 2

71

*** WIND SPEED IS ROOT-MEAN-SQUARE WIND SPEED
*** WET BULB IS CALCULATED FROM TEMPERATURE, DEW POINT AND PRESSURE

PROGRAM: TDP   VERSION: 3   DATED: MARCH 1982   RUN DATE: FRIDAY   MAY 7, 1982

SAMPLE RUN : INPUT FILE = DATA1   (SEE SAMPLE OUTPUT FOR PROGRAM PRINT)

YEAR MONTH		110.0 METERS				60.0 METERS				10.0 METERS			
		AVG	MIN	MAX	HRS	AVG	MIN	MAX	HRS	AVG	MIN	MAX	HRS
1980 DECEMBER	WIND SPEED (M/S)	10.8	1.0	18.0	37	9.3	0.1	40.0	36	12.1	1.0	20.0	27
	TEMPERATURE (C)	19.4	12.0	22.0	36	21.8	14.0	26.5	35	22.5	13.0	30.0	37
	DEW POINT (C)	16.0	10.0	21.0	37	999.9	99.9	-99.9	0	16.8	10.0	24.0	36
	WET BULB (C)	17.4	11.7	20.9	34	999.9	99.9	-99.9	0	19.3	13.4	24.3	36
1980 ANNUAL	WIND SPEED (M/S)	10.8	1.0	18.0	37	9.3	0.1	40.0	36	12.1	1.0	20.0	27
	TEMPERATURE (C)	19.4	12.0	22.0	36	21.8	14.0	26.5	35	22.5	13.0	30.0	37
	DEW POINT (C)	16.0	10.9	21.0	37	999.9	99.9	-99.9	0	16.8	10.0	24.0	36
	WET BULB (C)	17.4	11.7	20.9	34	999.9	99.9	-99.9	0	19.3	13.4	24.3	35

*** WIND SPEED IS ROOT-MEAN-SQUARE WIND SPEED
*** WET BULB IS CALCULATED FROM TEMPERATURE, DEW POINT AND PRESSURE

72

PROGRAM: TDP   VERSION: 3   DATED: MARCH 1982   RUN DATE: FRIDAY   MAY 7, 1982

SAMPLE RUN : INPUT FILE = DATA1   (SEE SAMPLE OUTPUT FOR PROGRAM PRINT)

YEAR MONTH		110.0 METERS				60.0 METERS				10.0 METERS			
		AVG	MIN	MAX	HRS	AVG	MIN	MAX	HRS	AVG	MIN	MAX	HRS
1981 JANUARY	WIND SPEED (M/S)	10.8	1.9	18.0	32	8.5	0.1	24.0	32	10.1	1.0	20.0	28
	TEMPERATURE (C)	18.2	12.0	22.0	33	20.0	14.0	26.5	31	20.4	13.0	30.0	33
	DEW POINT (C)	13.9	10.0	21.0	35	999.9	99.9	-99.9	0	17.3	10.0	24.0	35
	WET BULB (C)	15.7	11.7	20.9	32	999.9	99.9	-99.9	0	19.1	13.4	24.3	31
1981 ANNUAL	WIND SPEED (M/S)	10.8	1.0	18.0	32	8.5	0.1	24.0	32	10.1	1.0	20.0	28
	TEMPERATURE (C)	18.2	12.0	22.0	33	20.0	14.0	26.5	31	20.4	13.0	30.0	33
	DEW POINT (C)	13.9	10.0	21.0	35	999.9	99.9	-99.9	0	17.3	10.0	24.0	35
	WET BULB (C)	15.7	11.7	20.9	32	999.9	99.9	-99.9	0	19.1	13.6	24.3	31

*** WIND SPEED IS ROOT-MEAN-SQUARE WIND SPEED
*** WET BULB IS CALCULATED FROM TEMPERATURE, DEW POINT AND PRESSURE

PROGRAM: TDP   VERSION: 3   DATED: MARCH 1982   RUN DATE: FRIDAY   MAY 7, 1982

SAMPLE RUN : INPUT FILE = DATA1   (SEE SAMPLE OUTPUT FOR PROGRAM PRINT)

DECEMBER 30, 1980
        TO
JANUARY   2, 1981

	110.0 METERS				60.0 METERS				10.0 METERS			
	AVG	MIN	MAX	HRS	AVG	MIN	MAX	HRS	AVG	MIN	MAX	HRS
WIND SPEED (M/S)	10.8	1.0	18.0	69	5.9	0.1	40.0	68	11.3	1.0	20.0	59
TEMPERATURE (C)	18.8	12.0	22.0	69	21.0	16.0	26.5	65	21.5	13.0	30.0	72
DEW POINT (C)	15.0	10.0	21.0	72	999.9	99.9	-99.9	0	17.0	10.0	24.0	67
WET BULB (C)	16.6	11.7	20.9	66	999.9	99.9	-99.9	0	19.2	13.6	26.3	66

*** WIND SPEED IS ROOT-MEAN-SQUARE WIND SPEED
*** WET BULB IS CALCULATED FROM TEMPERATURE, DEW POINT AND PRESSURE

74

APPENDIX A

NRC STANDARD FORMAT FOR METEOROLOGICAL DATA

Use: 9 track tape (7 will be acceptable)
                Stnadard Label, which would include
                    Record Length = 160 characters
                    Block Size = 3200 characters (fixed block size)
                    Density = 1600 BPI preferred (6250 or 800 PBI will be
                                                  accepted)

Do not use: Magnetic tapes with unformatted or spanned records.

At the beginning of each tape, use the first five records (which is the
equivalent of ten cards) to give a tape description. Include plant name and
location (latitude, longitude), dates of data, information explaining data
contained in the "other" fields if they are used, height of measurements, and
any additional information pertinent to identification of the tape. Make sure
all five records are included, even if some are blank. Format for the first
five records will be 160A1. Meteorological data format is (I6, I2, I3, I4,
25F5.1, F5.2, 3F5.1). Decimal points should not be included when copying data
onto the tape.

All data should be given to a tenth of a unit except solar radiation, which
should be given to a hundredth of a unit. This does not necessarily indicate
the accuracy of the data (e.g., wind direction is usually given to the nearest
degree, but record it with a zero in the tenth's place; therefore, 275 degrees
would be 275.0 degrees and placed on the tape as 2750). All nines in any
field should indicate a lost record (99999). All sevens in a wind direction
field should indicate calm (77777). If only two levels of data are monitored,
use the upper and lower level fields. If only one level of data is monitored,
use the upper level field.

TABLE A-1

MAGNETIC TAPE METEORLOGICAL DATA

LOCATION:
DATE OF DATA RECORD:

		ACCURACY
I6	Identifier (can be anything)	
I2	Year	
I3	Julian Day	
I4	Hour (on 24-hr clock)	
F5.1	Upper Measurements: Level = _____ meters	
F5.1	Wind Direction (degrees)	_____
F5.1	Wind Speed (m/s)	_____
F5.1	Sigma Theta (degrees)	_____
F5.1	Ambient Temperature (°C)	_____
F5.1	Moisture: _____	_____
F5.1	Other: _____	_____
F5.1	Intermediate Measurements: Level = _____ meters	
F5.1	Wind Direction (degrees)	_____
F5.1	Wind Speed (m/s)	_____
F5.1	Sigma Theta (degrees)	_____
F5.1	Ambient Temperature (°C)	_____
F5.1	Moisture: _____	_____
F5.1	Other: _____	_____
F5.1	Lower Measurements: Level = _____ meters	
F5.1	Wind Direction (degrees)	_____
F5.1	Wind Speed (m/s)	_____
F5.1	Sigma Theta (degrees)	_____
F5.1	Ambient Temperature (°C)	_____
F5.1	Moisture: _____	_____
F5.1	Other: _____	_____
F5.1	Temp Diff (Upper-Lower) (°C/100 meters)	_____
F5.1	Temp Diff (Upper-Intermediate) (°C/100 meters)	_____
F5.1	Temp Diff (Intermediate-Lower) (°C/100 meters)	_____
F5.1	Precipitation (m.)	_____
F5.2	Solar Radiation (cal/cm^2/min)	_____
F5.1	Visibility (km)	_____
F5.1	Other: _____	_____
F5.1	Other: _____	_____